To Joseph,
With very best wish

And Smoking Flax Shall He Not Quench

Reflections on New Testament Themes

And Smoking Flax Shall He Not Quench

Reflections on New Testament Themes

THOMAS A. FAY

PARACLETE ● New York

AND SMOKING FLAX SHALL HE NOT QUENCH

Copyright © 1979 by THOMAS A. FAY

DEDICATED TO
MY BELOVED MOTHER
Who Rests in the Lord

Contents

Foreword

The collection of essays which follows, although rather loosely strung together, does have a certain unifying theme. This theme might be variously expressed, but what it really comes down to is something like this—seeing things as Jesus saw them, or, to use St. Paul's expression, to "Let that mind be in you which was also in Christ Jesus." This Christ-mind is revealed to us as we see the way in which Jesus spent his life, how he looked at the persons, events and situations which he encountered in his brief earthly stay. As we reflect on the life and teaching of Jesus we discover that the Christ-mind consisted in certain fundamental attitudes toward life, and that one of Jesus' principal purposes was to develop these same fundamental attitudes toward life in his followers. We have considered several, though certainly not all, of these basic attitudes toward life which Jesus taught both by word and the example of his life. These fundamental life positions, it is suggested, will lead us to the rich, full and abundant life that Jesus tells us in St. John's Gospel he came to give us.

The title of this collection of essays is taken from the last one in the group, for the reason that even though we see the various ways which Jesus proposes to us in the first nine essays by which we might achieve the abundant life he came to give us, most of us find that we are very slow in learning, and Penelope-like, busy ourselves unravelling what Jesus has, with such care and love, woven into our lives. These words then, "And smoking flax shall he not quench," which describe our Savior's solicitude for us, offer us great comfort and no little hope.

Finally, the King James Version of the Bible has been used throughout because of what I take to be the matchless beauty of its stately prose.

1 | Give and It Shall Be Given to You ...

Luke 6:38

On the question of human happiness George Bernard Shaw somewhere remarks with his customary piquancy, "The closest definition of hell would be a perpetual holiday." At first glance it seems a rather peculiar thing to say. I suppose all of us in some secret corner of our mind, at least at some point in our lives, have harbored the thought of how nice it would be to be rich enough to have everything we could want and do exactly what we pleased. In short, to be on a perpetual holiday. But if one stops to think the matter over more seriously, one comes to realize more and more that there is a very solid kernel of truth in what Shaw says. But why should this be so? What is there about human happiness that the more we pursue it, the less we are able to find it? Or, to put the question a different way, the way Jesus did, "The man who seeks his life will lose it. The man who loses his life for my sake will find it." Implicit in the statement of Jesus are two different, diametrically opposed approaches to life. The first, a way which seems preemptively attractive, counsels us to seek for our happiness by doing those things, and only those, which will promote our self-interest. This is a way which ultimately leads to frustration and the type of disillusionment which some people who have pursued this course experience midway through life, described so vividly by Dante in the *Divine Comedy,* I, 1, when he writes, "In the middle of life's journey, I found myself in a dark forest, where I had lost my way." This way of an exclusionary self-seeking, is speciously attractive, but ultimately leads to misery, and if pursued strenuously enough, to solipsism and a tragic loneliness.

Thus, the first way of life which is open to man which Jesus epitomizes under the rubric of the "man who seeks his life." The other possibility which Jesus offers seems, at least at first glance, to be a singularly unattractive prospect. Thus Jesus says, "The man who loses his life for my sake will find it." This proposed way of life which Jesus would have us follow stands at antipodes to the first way. Instead of adopting as its basic posture toward life the "taker's" stance which seeks only for self, this approach is one of giving, or as Paul puts it, "Love . . . seeketh not for herself" (I Corinthians 13:5) . The insight which Jesus has expressed in this teaching that the man who seeks his life will lose it, and the man who loses his life for His sake will find it, reveals a strangely paradoxical aspect of human happiness. Happiness, it seems, if sought directly in itself forever eludes us. If we do not seek it, that is according to Jesus, if we lose our life for his sake, we will find it. But what does Jesus mean when he says "lose"?

The way the follower of Christ "loses his life" is the same way in which Jesus did—to give it away. Jesus has said the disciple is not greater than the Master. The disciple becomes a perfect disciple when he becomes like the Master (Matthew 10:24-25) . When the prospective disciple of Jesus studies the life of the Master with a view to finding out what were its characteristics so that he might emulate them, he discovers

that Jesus' purpose in coming into the world was not
to receive anything, not to get or to take anything,
but rather to *give*. Jesus states quite clearly, "The son
of Man has not come to be served, but to *serve,* to *give*
his life as a ransom" (Matthew 20:28). If one wishes
to be a follower of Christ, then, the basic attitude toward life which one adopts ought to be as much like
that of Jesus as possible. That is, the fundamental approach should be that of giving and service, as this
was the basic approach to life of Jesus.

This approach is also called by Jesus "seeking the
kingdom of God and his righteousness." And in terms
of the question of human happiness, or "finding one's
life" (or to use the current phrase "finding oneself") ,
this is why Jesus directs us to, "Seek ye first the kingdom of God, and his righteousness; and all these things
shall be added unto you" (Matthew 6:33). In other
words, what Jesus is saying with regard to happiness is
that we should not seek our happiness directly, as an
end in itself, at least insofar as this is understood to
mean the goods which we hope will bring us happiness,
but rather that happiness is a kind of "spinoff," so to
speak, from seeking something else, that is the "Kingdom of God." Now by seeking the Kingdom of God
we are to understand adopting Jesus' attitude toward
life, since this was the basic purpose of his life. That
is to say, we are to "Let that mind be in us which was
also in Christ Jesus," which in its turn means to conceive of our lives as Jesus did his—in terms of giving
and service. And it is in just such a giving attitude

that we are able to achieve happiness, though achieving happiness is not what our primary aim is in giving. Happiness comes as a kind of "fringe benefit." This is why Jesus says, "Give and it shall be given to you." There is a kind of inexhaustibleness in generous giving which springs from love.

We see a very beautiful symbol of this in the First Book of Kings in the Old Testament. We are told that a great famine has spread over the land and the people are starving. The prophet Elijah, who is also starving, goes to the city of Zarepath and at the city gate we are told that he encounters a widow who is gathering a few sticks together so that she can go home and build a fire to bake a hearth cake with her last few grains of flour which are all that stand between her and her son and starvation. Elijah calls out to her and asks her to bring him a drink of water, and when she agrees he calls after her to bring him also a morsel of food. The widow answers him by saying that she has only a handful of flour and a few drops of oil, and that even now she is going home to use it to make their last scanty meal for her and her son before they die like everyone else in the city of starvation. But Elijah says to her, "Fear not: go and do as thou has said: but make me thereof a little cake first, and bring in unto me, and after make for thee and thy son. For thus saith the Lord God of Israel, the barrel of meal shall not waste, neither shall the cruse of oil fail, until the day that the Lord sendeth rain upon the earth" (I Kings 17:13-14). The widow did as Elijah requested, and true to His promise, God rewarded this act of generous giving by not allowing the grain or oil to be exhausted. And so during the long days of the famine the widow was able to feed herself, her son and the prophet from this same grain and oil and in giving it away it was not diminished.

Here we see a beautiful symbol of the limitless inexhaustibility of a generous spirit. This is expressed in a very charming way in the famous couplet of John Bunyon.

> *"A man there was and they called him mad,*
> *And the more he gave, the more he had."*

According to this view, giving, far from diminishing the giver, actually replenishes in the very giving. And here we see a strongly paradoxical facet of giving. When we share our goods we are not diminished but enriched in the giving; while when sorrows are shared they are lessened. Thus the wisdom of the old saying that goods shared are doubled; while sorrows shared are halved.

This is why Jesus can say, "Give and it shall be given to you." Unfortunately, many of us would prefer to follow the conventional wisdom, saying to ourselves, "After I get, then I shall give," or as they say, "show me the color of your money and I will show you the color of my service." But unfortunately this niggardly attitude towards life results in a very impoverished life. People of this persuasion are very much like the hiker who was caught in an unforeseen blizzard and after hours of trudging half frozen through the snow finally chanced upon an abandoned cabin, and after entering and pulling a chair close to the pot-bellied stove he insisted stubbornly, "You give me heat. Then I'll put wood in you." All to frequently our attitude toward life makes just as little sense as this. This is why Jesus insisted that we adopt a different approach —that as we give to life, so life will give back to us.

Jesus also teaches this using a different, an agricultural analogy. He tells us that the sower went out to sow and that the seed which was sown yielded a harvest that was rich in proportion to what was sown. Where the sowing had been abundant, so also was the harvest; where the sowing was meagre, the yield was also correspondingly scanty. Again Jesus, gives us the same teaching in the parable of the talents. In St. Matthew's Gospel Jesus likens the kingdom of heaven to a man who went off on a far journey, and at his departure confided his goods to his servants. To one he gave five talents, to another two, and to another one. The first servant went and traded diligently and earned another five; the second did likewise and gained an additional two for his master; the third wrapped his in a handkerchief and dug a hole and buried it in the ground. Upon his return the master exacted a reckoning of his servants. The first one told the master how he had gone out and traded diligently with the five talents that had been entrusted to his keeping and had succeeded in gaining an additional five, so that the master had his capital back with 100% interest. Needless to say, he was pleased. So also the second servant who had received two talents was able to return the principle with a 100% interest rate. Again, the master was delighted. When, however, he came to the third servant, he was very angry. This third servant, because of his attitude toward life, had gained nothing at all for his master, there had been no enrichment at all because of his attitude of holding back. And then at the conclusion of this parable we read words that at first glance seem very difficult to understand, but which are the key to understanding what the basic intent of the teaching contained in this parable is. The master then directs the attendants to take the one talent away from the third servant and to give it to the one who has ten already. The first reaction of many people to this is to cry, "Foul! The master is unfair! Why, doesn't this fellow already have ten? Why should he get it? The poor man who has only one, and now none at all, certainly seems to need it much more than the man who has ten talents already." The concluding lines of the parable are most interesting. After the one talent has been taken from the man the master gives as his reason for acting in this way, "For unto everyone that hath shall be given, and he shall have in abundance: but from him that hath not shall be taken away even that which he hath" (Matthew 25:28) . The point that Jesus wishes to make here is exactly the same one that is made when he says, "Give and it shall be given to you," and, "with what measure you measure it will be measured unto you." The first servant took his God given talents and gave of them, as did the second, and in proportion as they gave did they receive back in return. The miserly approach to life of the third servant who did not trade with his talent, that is, take his God given abilities and use them in the service of God and his fellow man, but buried them, that is, selfishly clung to them refusing to give of them, resulted in the loss of even that which he had. So what Jesus is saying in this parable is that if we refuse to give, we also will reap no harvest of happiness.

It is a most comforting thought also to remember the return which God makes to us for our giving is in no way proportionate to our gift. Put differently, God will not be outdone in generosity. That is why Jesus goes on to add, "Give, and it shall be given unto you; good measure, pressed down, and shaken together and running over, shall men give into your bosom." (Luke 6:38). God won't shortchange us in this exchange. Rather, we shall receive "good measure." This is, of course, not to say, and let us repeat it, that the giver *aims at* the reward in giving. No, the gift is given with no thought of reward. The reward simply comes as the inevitable consequence of the good act. A mother, for example, in giving of herself to nurse a sick child certainly has no thought in her mind about how such an act is ennobling and enriching her soul, although without her ever noticing it this is surely happening. Her sole concern is for the sick child, and so she watches through the long hours of the night at the bedside, even when she can do nothing directly to allay the child's suffering. Somehow, she feels, the child needs her, if only her presence, to share the pain, even though she can do nothing else. As one observes this scene one is moved by the sublime moral beauty of such an act. The mother, no doubt, is completely unaware of the spiritual transformation which her response to this spiritual value is bringing to pass but though she is unaware it is still happening and her soul grows in its response to this call of value. Indeed, to use Jesus' expression, she gets "good measure," for the spiritual growth and enrichment which takes place is even greater than what she may be able to do. Her approach to life here is in terms of giving—she gives generously, and she receives even more. If we contrast a life lived out of such a basic attitude with one which is spent merely in the quest of self-gratification, the incomparably greater richness of the one over the other becomes quite apparent. Another woman, let us say, motivated only by her own selfish interests, leaves her children to fend for themselves while she pursues her own interests of bridge, golf and a ceaseless round of club activities. She gets very little out of being a mother, except what she perceives to be inconveniences and annoyances, because she gives very little. At the conclusion of such a life we notice that the spiritual beauty and nobility which were drawn forth from the soul of the first is noticeably lacking in the second. Instead, what we perceive is a person who is encapsulated in a hard and impenetrable veneer of egoncentricity.

Again, when Jesus says give and it shall be given to you, this giving can take another form which is also of the very greatest importance in developing those attitudes of mind which are vitally important to man in his quest for happiness. The form of giving that we have in mind here is *thanks-giving*. We read in St. Luke's Gospel that one day as Jesus was traveling toward Jerusalem he passed through a Samaritan village, and as he passed, ten lepers, keeping their distance because of their uncleanness, cried out, "Jesus, Master, have mercy on us" (Luke 17:13). Jesus took pity on them and healed them, commanding them to go show themselves to the priests, as the law required. As they followed his command and were going to the priests they discovered that they had been healed. One of them, moved by a deep sense of gratitude for what Jesus had done for him, returned and fell on his face at Jesus' feet, giving him thanks. At which Jesus remarked, "Were not ten cleansed? But where are the other nine?" Now as we read this statement of Jesus it raises a certain question. Why does Jesus ask about the nine ungrateful lepers, who, cured from this terrible disease, never even so much as came back to say thanks? After all, why should Jesus care? Did he cure them in order to experience the human satisfaction of having people who were indebted to him fawning over him in fulsome thanks? No, of course this was not the case. Rather, by this miracle Jesus is recommending to us the necessity of what he takes to be a fundamental moral attitude—gratitude, and the expression of gratitude in thanksgiving. Jesus by his question, "where are the other nine?" implicitly condemns their ingratitude, not because he needs to be thanked, and feels hurt and unappreciated. Jesus knows that they should give thanks for the gift which they have received not because *He* needs it, but because *they do*. And the reason for this is because of all the human attitudes that are most likely to conduce to our happiness, there is none quite so important as this type of giving—*thanksgiving*.

The reason for this is really quite simple. Philosophers have, since time immemorial, reflected on this most central of human concerns—happiness—what is it? how does one achieve it? During the long history of Philosophy, beginning with Socrates, various definitions of happiness have been proposed. Aristotle in the *Ethics* seemed to think that it was a contemplative activity. Boethius in the sixth century A.D. in his famous work *On the Consolation of Philosophy* defined it as a state made perfect by the aggregate of all good things. Later on in the thirteenth century St. Thomas in *Summa Theologiae* defined it as a perfect good which fully brings to rest all of man's hopes, desires and aspirations. But however different the various definitions of happiness might be which have been formulated throughout the long history of Philosophy, certain parameters become evident, and when we collate these, the distillate of philosophic reflection on happiness seems to come down to this. Happiness is desire satisfied by conscious possession of the good. Regardless of their individual differences, most philosophers would at least agree to this. Now if it is true that happiness means desire satisfied by conscious possession of the good, this suggests that the crucial element in happiness is not so much the good, or aggregate of goods which we possess, be these expensive cars, beautiful yachts, money in abundance, or whatever. Rather, where happiness is concerned, what is quintessentially important is our *attitude,* that is, the attitude of taking delight in the good which we possess. The mere fact of possessing a beautiful home, a fine car, having wonderful children, a rewarding career, excellent health, is not sufficient to make us happy. What is crucial, is one's attitude toward these goods. If one merely takes it all for granted, then it is certain that they are not going to generate even a spark of happiness.

An example may serve to illustrate the point. Some years ago in England there was a blind man who had a seeing-eye dog. One day when he was in his bedroom which was on the second story of his house he went to go into the bathroom and being unaware that his dog was lying across the doorway, tripped over him and fell headlong down the stairs, landing at the bottom and striking his head a very severe blow. As he regained consciousness, he opened his eyes—and miracle of miracles, he could see! How do you suppose he felt? Well, one would, no doubt, be hard-pressed to find adequate descriptives. But one thing is certain—he most certainly was happy beyond measure. But why?

Of course, because he could see. But it can't simply be the good which he now possesses of seeing which makes one happy. After all, everyone who is reading this book can see. Are you as happy as the man who has just recovered his sight? Why not? You and I, we have the same good which the former blind man has, and which makes him happy beyond description. So we see it is not just possessing a good which makes one happy, whether it is eyesight or something else. The man who was blind and now can see is happy because he takes such delight in this good that he is beside himself. For the average person who has enjoyed this miraculous gift of God called sight all of his life it is simply something that we take for granted and no special occasion for rejoicing.

From this it seems clear that it is not so much the good which we possess which makes us happy, but rather our attitude toward it. The question is, is our attitude toward our life and all the gifts which God has given us one of delight, or do we just take everything for granted? When our attitude as we open our eyes in the morning, is like the attitude of the blind man when he opened his on the bottom of the stairs, then we are on our way to happiness. When we open our eyes in the morning and see each day as a new miracle and greet it with awestruck wonder, then we are also on the way to becoming happy. It was for this reason that Jesus said of the Lepers, "Where are the other nine?" It wasn't because *he* needed their thanks. It was because *they* did. The man who was cured and returned, who was so overwhelmed with a sense of gratitude that he threw himself on his face on the ground at the feet of Jesus, was happy. Why? Because having been deprived of health for so many years, having suffered from the pain of the progressive rotting away of his flesh, and having had to suffer all of this in isolation, deprived of human company, when he was healed, he felt so grateful that he didn't know what to do except throw himself on his face in gratitude and worship the person who healed him. A man who feels like that is a happy man.

But what of the other nine? They apparently felt no gratitude, not even enough to return for a "thank you." When they wake up the next day will they greet that day as a new miracle? No, certainly not. The new day is not a fresh and dazzling gift of God for them, as it will be for the Leper who showed his gratitude by his thanks. For them it will just be "another day." And one of the very sad and sobering things about this healing of the Lepers is the mathematics involved. One gets the feeling in reading this story that it is not only with lepers that nine out of ten feel no gratitude. One has the feeling that Jesus is saying that is how it is with the human race in general.

Jesus is trying to teach us a very important lesson here and one that has crucially important implications for the question of our happiness. Jesus came that we might have life, and not just life as a day to day drudgery, of somehow "hanging in there," as they say. He came that we might have abundant life, a rich, full, satisfying life. He knew that in order for us to achieve this we have to do something, we have to *give*, if we wish to receive. We must not be like the man sitting in front of the stove stubbornly insisting that the stove give him heat and then he will give the stove wood. No, we have to act with faith in Jesus' words, "Give and it shall be given to you." And we need have no fear God will be outdone in generosity. He will give us "good measure," and more, "pressed down, shaken together until it runs over." If we adopt this as our basic posture toward life we will have the abundant life Jesus promised. And if we not only give, but *thanks-give,* as Jesus teaches us, we will not only receive his gifts abundantly but in constantly giving thanks for them we will be growing day by day in that attitude which is necessary above all others for experiencing true happiness.

2 | *My Yoke Is Easy and My Burden Light ...*

Matthew 11:30

In one of the best known, and certainly one of the most beautifully poetic texts in the entire Scripture, Jesus addresses these poignant words to us, "Come unto me, all ye that labor and are heavy laden, and I will give you rest. Take my yoke upon you, and learn of me; for I am meek and lowly in heart: and ye shall find rest unto your souls. For my yoke is easy, and my burden is light" (Matthew 11:28-30). No doubt one of the reasons for the universality of the appeal of these words of Jesus is because we can all so easily identify with them. Who is there that does not at times feel crushed under the weight of life's burdens? Who is there that does not at times feel overwhelmed by problems, the cares, the responsibilities of life whether they come to us in the form of marriage problems, a cold, unloving, unresponsive husband; children with whom we no longer seem to be able to communicate and who seem at times to be total strangers; a wife who seems totally to lack appreciation and sympathetic understanding for the mental anguish of her husband who is both crushed under the weight of financial worries and who is hopelessly stuck in a job which he hates; those who suffer from the pains of loneliness; those who experience the suffering of sickness—in short, all who feel "The heart-aches and the thousand natural shocks that flesh is heir to," as Shakespeare puts it so beautifully.

To all of weary humanity, whatever the burdens they bear, Jesus addresses his words of comfort. Jesus invites us to take up his yoke, but in order to take up the yoke of Jesus we must learn of him. What was Jesus like that his yoke, that is the way of life to which he invites us, should be easy, his burden light? Certainly the external circumstances of Jesus' life were not leisurely, easy, or free from care. He traveled constantly, on foot, from one end of Palestine to the other; he was constantly engaged in teaching, preaching, healing the sick from daybreak till dark, and even when darkness came and he attempted to steal away for a few quiet moments of repose, the people sought him out. We are told by Mark, for example, that the crowds made such demands on Jesus that he had no time so much as even to eat (Mark 6:31) . And even here when he tried to slip away to refresh his spirit in prayer the people see him and ". . . ran afoot thither out of all cities, and outwent them, and came together unto him." Nor could the compassionate heart of Jesus turn the crowds away for he, "Was moved with pity toward them, because they were as sheep not having a shepherd. . ." (Mark 6:34) .

All of which suggests a quite perplexing paradox, that is, if we study the life of Jesus, judged at least from its externals, it seems to have been a life that was far from being free from cares, and labors, but was rather a life of almost ceaseless, and indeed at times such as those mentioned above, almost frantic, activity. Well, the paradox is this—if Jesus himself labored so constantly and unremittingly, and was the center of such a maelstrom of activity, he seems hardly to be the model after whom we ought to pattern our lives, if we are seeking "rest unto our souls" from all of life's busy and wearying labor. Still, Jesus does state that we are to learn of him if we wish to find rest and repose for our souls. The answer to this seeming contradiction of a man who is embroiled in such feverish activity that he hardly has breathing space to catch a bite to eat suggesting that we model our lives on his if we wish to find rest and peace for our hearts lies in this—that regardless of how hectic Jesus' activity might seem when looked at from the outside, at the center of Jesus' life was a deep peace and calm. This undisturbed center of Jesus' life was produced by singleness of purpose. And that purpose which gave unity and coherence to the manifold activities of Jesus may be summarized in one simple word— love. A love which impels him to spend his life and himself for others. Thus Jesus says of his purpose in coming into the world, that he came not to be served but to serve and to offer his life as a ransom (Matthew 20:28). And the captors from whom we must be ransomed are our selfishness and egocentricity. The answer, then, to the seeming incongruity of Jesus, so totally immersed in activity that it would seem he must be totally exhausted by it, offering himself as a model for those who would find rest for their souls may be found in this—that it is not the multiplicity of external activities that wears one out, provided that those activities are held together by, and rotate around the centripetal force of a unified, transcendent purpose. Without such an attractive center of love which draws all of life's events, situation and activities to it so that they might share in the intelligibility of this purpose, all of the events, persons and actions of our life tend to be governed by centrifugal forces which pull them chaotically into a patternless space. It is activity of this sort which exhausts us and dissipates our interior strength, and not activity per se, regardless of how strenuous, regardless of how demanding.

In this connection, the life of St. Augustine is very instructive. In his mature years, looking back over his life, on the opening pages of his *Confessions* (I, 1), Augustine is led to remark, "Because you have created us for yourself, O Lord, our hearts are restless till they rest in thee." In his youth Augustine had followed many of the well-trodden paths which have, since time immemorial, held out the hope of human happiness. He had sought to achieve happiness through fame, and did indeed achieve great fame as a rhetorician. He had attempted to achieve happiness through sensual pleasure, and had left the African coast and the Italian peninsula strewn with abandoned mistresses and illegitimate children, one of whom he had named, with a disarming simplicity, Adeodatus, the gift of God. But in all of these questings he had not found happiness, but only *inquietum,* a restlessness which wearied him. It was only when Augustine tried a different road, one which pointed toward God, that he was able to find the rest for his soul that he longed for. Once God became the center of his life, he could, following the example of Jesus, spend himself unstintingly in the love of God. When his center became the love of God, he could then expend himself inexhaustibly in a life dedicated to the service of his brothers and sisters in the Lord. So Augustine, in spite of his numberless activities, whether of writing, or of preaching, whether in the endless administrative work of a bishop, or in his concern for the "cura animarum," the care of souls, could still be at peace, and in the midst of these multifarious labors find rest for his soul. The reason for this is clear enough. Because he had found God, God had given a unified purpose to his life, and regardless of how frenzied the activities might become, his soul had found its calm and peaceful center.

If, then, we feel worn out with life's cares and problems and responsibilities, if we feel way-worn from our endless strivings, perhaps Augustine's experience may prove helpful for us. It is not work in itself which wears one out. Augustine, who as a young man of about thirty was already very weary, after his conversion, far from retrenching his activities in order to find the peace which he was seeking, increased them tenfold. And in spite of this, found refreshment for his soul. Why? Because now he was no longer motivated by an enervating egocentricity selfishly seeking only what was good for himself. Instead, he is now moved by a vitalizing transcendent purpose, the love of God and the service of his brothers and sisters in the Lord which is the expression of this love. It is only such a transcendent purpose which can free one from the narrow confines of the self-imposed prison which the self builds for itself through seeking only itself.

This, of course, was the tremendous insight which Jesus had when he uttered one of his most enigmatic statements—"Whosoever shall seek to save his life shall lose it; and whosoever shall lose his life shall preserve it" (Luke 17:33). That is to say, the more we selfishly seek for ourselves, the less real, satisfying happiness we will find. It is like trying to catch a beam of sunshine in our hand and hold it fast. It just can't be done. The spiritual law which governs our lives is a simple one— the more we selfishly seek for ourselves, the less really truly satisfying happiness we will find. And it is just such searching, that is, for what will benefit *me,* that produced the *taedium vitae,* a weariness with life which Augustine experienced, and which will also produce an ennui in ours. This is why Jesus says to all who experience this lassitude that they are to *learn of him.* And why? Because Jesus' life demonstrates in the clearest possible terms that it is not activity in itself which exhausts one, for Jesus' activity was ceaseless. Nor is it the absence of activity which in itself will produce rest for the soul, else all of the jaded jet-setters who have nothing else to do but please and amuse themselves would be abiding in deep peace, whereas there is every indication that what they most seem to feel is a suffocating boredom. So it is neither activity per se which wears us out, nor lack of it which produces peace for the soul, but rather something else, and this something else may be summarized in one word—love. This was the dynamo at the center of

Jesus' life which provided the energy for his number-less activities. It was also the driving force which was at the center of the life of an Augustine, a Paul in his indefatigable labors in establishing the nascent church, and which has been the vitalizing force in the life of every one of Christ's heroes and heroines throughout the ages, right down to our own days where it shines with an almost blinding luminosity in the life of Mother Teresa.

It is love which makes all things possible, as the great Latin poet Vergil observed when he wrote, "Amor vincit omnia," love conquers all things. This also may be of assistance to us in trying to understand what Jesus meant in one of the most difficult of his utterances, but one which is at the same time central to his teaching. This occurs in the fifth chapter of Matthew's Gospel, during the course of the Sermon on the Mount, where Jesus states, "Ye have heard that it hath been said, an eye for an eye, and a tooth for a tooth: But I say unto you, that ye resist not evil: but whoever shall smite thee on thy right cheek, turn to him the other also. And if any man will sue thee at the law, and take away thy coat, let him have thy cloak also. And whoever shall compel thee to go a mile, go with him twain" (Matthew 5:38-43) . We say that this may be taken to be a central teaching of Jesus because it occurs in chapter five of Matthew's Gospel which is the opening of the Sermon on the Mount, which runs from chapter five through chapter seven, and in the judgment of all Scripture scholars constitutes the nucleus of Jesus' teaching. But as we noted, this is also one of the most perplexing of the teachings of Jesus, and apparently one that has been much misunderstood. It has been used, for example, by anti-war groups to argue the case for a universal prohibition of all war; by groups opposed to capital punishment; by those favoring unilateral disarmament and so on. Well, they may, of course, be right. Then again, others, also members of the Christian community, have argued that it simply doesn't make sense to require those individuals, and those countries, who by reason of their good will and humanitarian instincts would lay aside all defenses, to be the defenseless prey of those who would simply exploit their good will to advance their own vicious designs of self-aggrandizement. And so those who would allow what the medieval philosophers called "A blameless self-defense" (cf. for example, St. Thomas, *Summa Theologiae,* II.II, q. 64, a. 7) , while they have vindicated the rights of the innocent to defend themselves against unjust aggression, have nevertheless not felt too comfortable with this particular section of St. Matthew's Gospel.

And then there is a further difficulty about "turning the other cheek" and "going the extra mile," which Jesus advocates. He didn't do it himself! What are we suggesting, that there is a hypocritical streak in the life of Jesus just as there was in the Pharisees which he so roundly denounced? No, certainly not that. Rather, that the intent behind this teaching may be quite different from a mere superficial literal interpretation, as it is understood by the first of the groups mentioned above who would interdict all self-defense in the name of "turning the other cheek" and "going the extra mile."

We said that Jesus himself, in his own dealing with others, did not simply turn the other cheek to evil doers and give them free rein to prey upon the innocent. Take, for example, the incident described by John 2:14-16, the cleansing of the temple. Jesus did not simply "turn the other cheek" as it were, to the merchants who turned the temple into a stockyard where cattle and livestock are bought and sold, and into a money exchange where people haggle over the rate of currency exchange. Quite the contrary. John tells us that he made a scourge of ropes and beat them with it, threw tables over, dispersed the cattle and drove them headlong out of the temple. All of which sounds remarkably unlike merely passively "turning the other cheek." Or when the Pharisees accuse Jesus of casting out devils by the Devil, Jesus does not simply "turn the other cheek" and let their viciousness go by unchallenged. Rather, he calls them a generation of vipers, that is, the most poisonous of all reptiles that slither along the ground (Matthew 12:34), a manner of acting not easily confused with "turning the other cheek."

If, then, as seems clear from these instances, and from many similar ones, Jesus did not simply "turn the other cheek" in every situation, and if further Jesus was not guilty of a hypocritical inconsistency between his teaching and his life, how can we explain this teaching of "turning the other cheek" and "going the extra mile" on the one hand, and Jesus' conduct on the other? The answer to this would seem to be the deeper meaning of Jesus' teaching here in the fifth chapter of Matthew. This deeper meaning, the soul which gives life to it, is, so to say, the same essential animating force which makes the yoke of Jesus easy, his burden light—love. Therefore, when Jesus says, "Resist not evil: but whosoever shall smite thee on thy right cheek, turn to him the other also," he is not talking about specific, particularized disputes that we might get into with others. Rather, what he is enunciating is a much more generalized spiritual law, and that is that love is to be the center, the driving force of our life. This is Jesus' radical new way of life. The radical newness of this way of Jesus can be seen, for example, in the series of couplets in the fifth chapter of Matthew, each of which begin with the words, "Ye have heard that it was said by them of old time. . ." (verses 21, 27, 31, 33, 38, 43), that is, the old approach to life, which are then paired immediately with a corresponding radically new approach, each of which begins, "But I say unto you" (verse 22, 28, 34, 39, 44). The purpose behind each of these articulations of the new teaching of Jesus is to free his followers from the narrowness in their thinking, and correspondingly in the life-styles which spring from their thinking, and to open up to them new and unlimited vistas which will be rendered possible when love replaces a narrow and stultifying concept of duty as the center of their lives.

The teaching of verses 38-41 affords an admirable illustration of the liberating and enlarging power of Jesus' new approach to life. In verse 38 Jesus recalls for them the old teaching, which had structured their moral lives since their birth, and indeed of the Israelites since their exodus from Egypt. Thus we read in the Old Law in the *Book of Exodus*, "And if any mischief follow then thou shall give life for life, eye for eye, tooth for tooth, hand for hand, foot for foot, burning for burning, wound for wound, stripe for stripe" (Exodus 21:23-25). But Jesus realized that this eye-for-an-eye approach to life, while it may have served a useful, and indeed a moderating purpose once, was now bankrupt. He realized that revenge is too costly a luxury to permit ourselves. He understood that if we attempt to avenge ourselves on our enemy we may, or may not, succeed in hurting him. But one thing is certain beyond any shadow of a doubt, and that is we will hurt ourselves. The corrosive juices which are released within us by the desire for revenge must inevitably do their destructive work on our own souls. Revenge is much like grabbing a dagger by the blade. We may succeed in hitting our enemy over the head with the handle and hurting him, but when we have succeeded in doing so our own hand will be a mangled, bloody mess. Jesus understood this. As he saw it, the spirit of unrelenting revenge was about as efficient in human interactions as burning down the barn to get rid of the mice. Certainly, you do succeed in getting rid of the mice. But the price is awfully high. Perhaps, too, this is why the scripture says, "Vengeance is mine saith the Lord"—because He is the only one who can afford it.

Therefore, Jesus says in verse 38, "Ye have heard that it hath been said, an eye for an eye, and a tooth for a tooth: But I say unto you, that ye resist not evil: but whoever shall smite thee on thy right cheek turn to him the other also," that is, that our lives be governed not by petty, self-destructive desires for revenge which must in the long run turn their baneful forces back on ourselves, but rather that we change our way of thinking, that we put on the Christ-mind. This Christ-mind is not, to be sure, an important indulgence of the viciousness of those who would injure the innocent, as we have seen from Jesus' action in the temple. Rather, it is an approach to life motivated by a love which opens up the horizons of life beyond the narrow perspectives of petty revenge. We can see this clearly from Jesus' own life when in his dying moments we see the sublime beauty of an act of forgiveness which is an expression of love for another when Jesus forgives those who cause his suffering and death.

In this section of the Sermon on the Mount (Matthew 5:38-41) concerning "turning the other cheek" and "going the extra mile" the teaching which lies behind the surface, which has caused such vexation to so many, is actually a general spiritual law which doesn't really have anything to do with people hitting us on the cheek, taking us to court to get our coat away from us, or compelling us to walk two miles out of our way. What Jesus is really trying to show us is the way to a richer, fuller, more abundant life. Because of a narrow self-interest, which must in the final accounting be self-defeating, we have been locked into lives which we find are perhaps boring, uninteresting, unsatisfactory, wearying. Jesus wants to show us a new way, a way that will lead to a fulfilling, interesting, abundant life. When He says "turn the other cheek," "go the extra mile" etc., the lesson he is trying to drive home to us by these deliberately provocative statements is a very simple one. Out attitude toward life should be one of generous giving, not a miserly attitude of "skimming it off the top." This is what Jesus is trying to teach us in all of these statements. We are to approach life with a generous spirit of giving, not just to content ourselves with doing the minimum. If we sow sparingly, our harvest in human happiness must also be similarly scanty. As Jesus tells us in Luke's Gospel, "Give and it shall be given unto you. For with the same measure that ye mete withal it shall be measured to you again" (Luke 6:38).

When Jesus says to go the "extra mile" what he is talking about is our general attitude toward life. How do we approach life? With what measure do we measure? How do we approach our work? Our neighbors? Our community? Are we content to do the minimum, to get by? What is our attitude toward our family? Is everything a burdensome duty that has to be gotten through somehow? How are we towards our wives and husbands? Is the birthday gift or Christmas gift, or anniversary gift (if we even remember it) simply something done *pro forma,* just an empty formality to get something or other in order to satisfy an obligation? How are we toward our work? Do we really have a generous attitude of giving something more than is absolutely required as a minimum, or is it strictly "take the money and run?"' Is our eye constantly on the clock, so that when 5 o'clock comes it looks like the starting break in the seventh race at Hialeah? What a commentary on the way we approach life we have in the famous initials which currently enjoy wide popular currency—T.G.I.F., "Thank-God-It's-Friday." What is crystalized in this popular expression is not just an attitude toward one's work, it is to be feared, but much more profoundly than that, it really indicates a basic, parsimonious attitude toward life itself which cannot but lead to a very impoverished kind of existence. Compare this "Thank-God-It's-Friday" way of life which leaves one so completely drained on Friday that one can only collapse in exhausted passivity in front of the television set, there to pass a boring and uncreative weekend, with the approach of those who really gave something to life and to their work. Could one imagine a Picasso who, when well into his nineties, still painted from early morning till late into the night saying at the close of the week, "Thank-God-It's-Friday"? Or could one imagine a Michelangelo lying on his back as he painted the ceiling of the Sistine Chapel impatiently cocking his ear to hear Friday's five o'clock whistle from the Vatican's smokestack, breathing with a sigh of relief, "Thank-God-It's Friday." No, we could not easily imagine that and the reason is very simple. The work of these men, and all who do really creative work whether they be shoemakers, bricklayers, salesmen, secretaries, housewives, or whatever, radiates from a vital and energizing center —love. They love, and because they love they give generously. And the more they give, the more they receive. The flinty-hearty, tight-fisted approach to life which will do no more than the absolute minimum leaves its practitioners so completely drained by the end of the week that they are incapable of anything except the desperate gasp, "Thank-God-It's-Friday."

Well, Jesus came to help just such people out—all of the "Thank-God-It's-Fridayers," and every one else that feels worn out and weary with life's burdens. And he offers them a rather strange and seemingly contradictory solution. Not to withdraw ourselves from activity, not to cut down on our activities, but rather to change their attitude to one of generous giving, to "go the extra mile." He invites all who are "heavy laden" to come to him. He promises all who come to him "rest unto their souls." He further promises all who come to him that his "yoke is easy his burden light." It is love which makes the yoke easy and the burden light. It is love which makes generous giving easy and natural, and our life a joy.

3 | Consider the Lilies of the Field ...

Matthew 6:28

Midway through the Sermon on the Mount, in which Jesus is laying out the broad principles of his teaching, he invites us to consider the fowls of the air who, "sow not, neither do they reap, nor gather into barns," and also the lilies of the field who "toil not, neither do they spin" (Matthew 6:26-30). Jesus goes on to point out that even though they are not concerned about providing for their future, God takes excellent care of them, and admonishes us that we ought to, "Take no thought for the morrow: for the morrow shall take thought for the things of itself" (Matthew 6:34). But this seems to be a quite strange teaching! In inviting us to learn a basic attitude toward life from the birds of the air and the flowers of the field, what is Jesus trying to tell us? It is surely quite evident to anyone who considers the matter that what may be true for birds and plants is most certainly not at all true for man. Lilies it is true, or at least so it would appear, do not concern themselves about their raiment. But it is also true if a late frost comes during the early spring night, in the morning they are all dead. Such an attitude would seem to have little in it to recommend it to man. The continuance of their species is also a relatively simple matter, at least when compared to man. The fertilized seeds falls into the ground and the matter is finished. The "mother" lily doesn't have to worry about providing food for its offspring, nor is the new offspring in any way dependent on its progenitor. With man, however, the case is quite different. For years the offspring is totally dependent on the parent for all of its basic needs: food, clothing, shelter, and of course what is perhaps the most primordial *human* need, love and affection. If the lily encounters a relatively chilly spring evening, it folds up its petals and waits for the warming morning sun. If an uncared for, unclothed baby is left in the cold all night it catches pneumonia and dies. Well, what this seems to suggest is that when Jesus tells us that we ought to consider the lilies of the field if we wish to get a better insight into how to approach life, it really doesn't seem that we can learn all that much from the life of the lilies. If all of this seems apparent enough, one is led to ask what the intent behind the teaching of Jesus can be. Is Jesus suggesting that human beings can grow like plants?

That, of course, was not his intent. Indeed a presumptuousness which takes no thought at all for life constituted one of the Devil's temptations which Jesus rejected earlier on in St. Matthew's Gospel. It will be recalled that the tempter took Jesus to the pinnacle of the temple and invited him to throw himself off, since Scripture states that, "He shall give his angels charge concerning thee: and in their hands they shall bear thee up, lest at any time thou dash thy foot against a stone. Jesus said unto him, It is written again, Thou shalt not tempt the Lord thy God" (Matthew 4:6-7). In interpreting Jesus' teaching of "take no thought for the morrow" we should be quite careful not to give it the sense of a reckless presumptuousness, an attitude which is explicitly considered by Jesus as a temptation of the Devil, and rejected. Rather this teaching forms part of the general teaching begun in verse 19 of this same sixth chapter which begins with the words, "Lay not up for yourselves treasures upon earth, where moth and rust doth corrupt, and where thieves break in and steal" (Matthew 6:19). The basic teaching here, that is from verse 19 through to the end of the chapter, is that man ought not to be *unduly* concerned about the day to day problems of making provision for his life. Jesus is in no way suggesting that we take no care whatever for our life. Nor is he suggesting to any-one, and love the other; or else he will hold to the one, visions for the future by saving our money when he says, "Lay not up for yourselves treasures upon earth." Rather, this must be understood in the light of what is for Jesus a fundamental principle in the approach to life that he would inculcate in us, when he says, "No man can serve two masters for either he will hate the one, and love the other; or else he will hold to the one, and despise the other. Ye cannot serve God and mammon" (Matthew 6:23). By this Jesus does not mean that if we are to be a true follower of his we must reject money and the material goods which it will buy, and divest ourselves of all of our possessions forthwith, and live like a lily of the field. Man cannot do that, and for a very good reason—he's not a lily!

If the human species is to continue *as human,* money, and the material goods which it will purchase, not only food and clothing, but books, violins, paintings, tapestries, sculpture and all of the other elements which are required for human culture, is necessary as a medium of exchange, at least barring a rapid return to the barter system, an event which seems exceedingly unlikely at this juncture of human history. So while Jesus is not recommending to us that we throw our money away, the intent of the teaching in verse 24 that we cannot serve God and money is not only a valid one, but one that has the very greatest importance for us in our approach to life. Notice that Jesus does not say that we cannot *have* money. What he says is that we should not *serve* money (or mammon). And this is a very useful and salutary corrective. For things being what they are, in our day to day struggle to eke out a living and make ends meet, there is the ever present danger that we might become so preoccupied with the acquisition of necessary wealth that we forget its purpose, that is, that we forget that it is a means and make it into an end in itself. In other words, that instead of money serving us, we find ourselves serving money. But Jesus came to set us free, and to use his expression, to offer his life as a ransom so that we might be freed from our captors. And one of these potential captors is money. But to *serve* any material thing is beneath human dignity, and it is this that Jesus would have us avoid.

When Jesus advises us that we might learn something quite valuable from the birds of the air and the lilies of the field he is not suggesting that we chuck everything and beat a swift retreat to the woods, there to grow, and let our children grow, like unspoiled wildflowers. He is not suggesting this for the very good reason that man is a human person and needs infinitely more nurturing than a flower if he is to achieve the full human potential of which he is capable. Rather, Jesus is trying to teach us a fundamental attitude toward life which is of inestimable value to man in his quest for happiness, and his teaching is this. On the one hand we are surely not counselled to be reckless or imprudent. This is clearly not the meaning of, "Lay not up for yourselves treasures upon earth," (verse 19), nor of, "Behold the fowls of the air: for they sow not, neither do they reap, nor gather into barns. . ." (verse 26). This is most certainly not an exhortation to improvidence or profligacy. In the Old Testament, for example, the patriarch Joseph who followed a quite different course of action and not only sowed and reaped but also "gathered into barns" a seven year supply of grain to sustain the people during the impending lean years is commended for his prudence (Genesis, 41). When Jesus tells us to "take no care for the morrow," then, this is not to be understood as a mandate to throw away the ordinary means which are required for our own welfare or for that of our families, but rather as a teaching whose purpose is to help us to avoid excessive worry and anxiety about our welfare. Certainly, we are to do today whatever is reasonable to provide for tomorrow. Therefore, when God warned the patriarch Joseph through a dream of the impending famine, Joseph did not just sit back and enjoy the abundance of the seven years of rich harvest preceding it, heedless of the future. Quite the contrary. God not only warned him of the seven lean years but also advised him to make haste during the seven years of plenty to store up in barns provisions against the days of want that would surely follow. So what Jesus wishes to teach us here is not a reckless improvidence, but rather we are to avoid anxiety and an *over*concern for the future. In other words, we are to trust in God. And just as the lily is rooted in the soil and draws its sustenance from it quite naturally and effortlessly, and because of this need not concern itself about the future, so also man who is created by God and rooted in him as in the ground of his being need not fear for the future, for the God who created him and sustains him today, will protect and care for him tomorrow as well. The basic intent, then, of this teaching of Jesus concerning the lilies of the field is to recommend to us a total and unconditional trust in God.

This fundamental attitude in which we live in the present moment, doing whatever it requires, and confiding the future with complete trust to God's loving care is further brought out in what is, without doubt, the most basic of all Jesus' teachings, The Lord's Prayer. St. Luke tells us in the eleventh chapter of his Gospel that the disciples came to Jesus with the request, "Lord, teach us to pray" (Luke 11:1). The followers of Jesus who seemed to be forever making invidious comparisons to John's disciples, complained to Jesus that John's disciples seemed to be quite expert in the matter of prayer, while they seemed to be getting left in the lurch. So Jesus agreed to teach them to pray, and what is no doubt the most famous of all prayers followed, as Jesus said, "When ye pray, say, Our Father which art in heaven, Hallowed be thy name. Thy kingdom come. Thy will be done, as in heaven, so in earth. Give us day by day our daily bread. . ." (Luke 11:2-3). But what a curious prayer! "Give us *day by day* our daily bread". Here the disciples were expecting a *good* prayer, one with which they could easily out class John's disciples in their next prayer competition, and what does Jesus give them for a prayer? "Give us *day by day* our daily bread". Why didn't Jesus say, when you pray to our Father in heaven, say to Him, "Father, give us a guarantee of a *life time* supply of bread." That would have been a *good* prayer. Or even, "Father, give us our *yearly* supply of bread," not quite so good, but still, on the whole, pretty fair. Or at least, "Father give us this week our weekly supply of bread." Then at least they could ask Him on the Sabbath and be finished for the week. But, no, that is not the way Jesus wanted his followers to pray. Each day, and everyday, they are to ask their heavenly Father, "Father, give us this day our daily bread." Not bread enough for a year, nor bread enough for a week—just bread enough for today. But why should Jesus teach us to pray in this way? Well, it goes back again to the teaching of his which we have been considering. "Take no thought for the morrow: for the morrow shall take thought for the things of itself." In other words even here in the Lord's Prayer Jesus is subtly making what is for him, apparently, a point of central importance—don't trouble yourself about tomorrow! "Sufficient unto the day is the evil thereof" (Matthew 6:34). What Jesus is saying is that we are to live one day at a time. We cannot relive yesterday; that is irretrievably gone. We cannot live tomorrow. Indeed, given the vicissitudes to which human life is prey, we have no assurance that there will *be* a tomorrow, so there certainly isn't any point in worrying about it. In order, therefore, to drive the point home to us as forcefully as possible, that is of living in today, and not worrying about the past which is gone, and the future which is not yet, Jesus makes this idea a key element in the prayer which he gives his disciples.

In so doing, Jesus has several purposes in mind. One of the purposes it seems that this teaching that we are to ask each day for whatever we need for our life, symbolized in the bread, is to bring us peace of mind. If we live just *this day*, not yesterday, not tomorrow or the next day, we will find that this is a marvelous cure for worry. Yesterday is gone, we can't change it. We may have made mistakes, even done vicious, mean and hurtful things which we now bitterly regret. But we can't change it. Self-recrimination and self-flagellation over our past sins and mistakes is totally futile. Worrying or gnawing guilt feelings over our past wrongs are simply wasted effort, and a painful one at that, that serves no useful purpose. If we are sorry, God forgives us, and since God loves us we should love ourselves enough to forgive ourselves. Hence there is no point in worrying about the past. Nor is there any point in worrying about the future. That is totally in God's hands. Certainly we attempt to shape the future according to our hopes and aspirations, by performing those actions in the present, today, which we judge will help to make our goals a reality. But there are limits to what we can do, and so after we have done everything within our power to make our dreams come true, the rest we confide to God's hands with the utmost confidence, and by so doing worry and anxiety over the future are replaced by a deep sense of peace. We experience in our lives the beautiful words of the Book of Wisdom 3:1, "The souls of the just are in the hand of the Lord."

Another of the purposes which Jesus seems to have had in mind when he taught that we should ask each day for our daily bread is to build up our trust in him day by day. This is achieved because as we ask each day for that day's bread, we come to realize more and more that we are totally dependent on God, not only for bread, but for life itself. Now while at first glance the deep realization of our radical metaphysical contingency, that is our total dependence on God even for our existence itself, might seem a rather scary prospect, the opposite is really the case. When we truly understand this, then we become like the lilies. That is, we realize that if we owe our existence itself to God, and totally depend on him for it at every moment, why then relatively minor matters such as food, clothing, shelter, our future with the corporation, how our children will turn out, where we will get the money to pay the mortgage, etc., may be placed in God's hands with complete confidence, after we have made whatever human efforts which we can to assure the desired outcome.

The lesson of complete trust in God through the realization of total dependence on Him was also one of the very first ones which God taught His people. After God had freed the Israelites from their bondage in Egypt and they had crossed the Red Sea, they were forced to wander for forty years in the desert. Now when you stop to think about it this is rather strange because when the Israelites crossed the Red Sea they were probably no more than about 150 miles from where they finally wound up in the Promised Land, a distance they could have covered with a forced march in about a week. Why did it take them forty years to cover a distance that could have been traversed in a week? Why did God keep them wandering around out in the desert all that time? And another curious note, during their wanderings in the desert the only food which they had to eat was something called manna which God gave them each day. Thus we read in the Book of Exodus 16:4, "Then said the Lord unto Moses, behold, I will rain bread from heaven for you: and the people shall go out and gather a certain rate every day, that I may prove them. . ." Notice the way in which God chooses to deal with His people—they are to gather a certain rate *every day*. Further, if they attempt to store any of it up, it will rot. Thus we are told, "And Moses said, Let no man leave it till the morning. Notwithstanding they hearkened not unto Moses: but some of them kept of it until the morning, and it bred worms, and stank . . ." (Exodus 16: 19-20). Here we see in God's way of feeding His chosen people in the desert something that bears a striking similarity to what Jesus teaches in the Lord's Prayer. Why didn't God rain down on the Israelites provisions that would have been sufficient for a month, or at least a week, so that they could have avoided the inconvenience of having to go out every morning to gather it up? Apparently the Jews themselves felt the same way about the matter and attempted at least in the beginning, to lay in a few days supply so that they could catch a few extra winks in the morning, since they had to gather it before sunrise. But it seems God had something different in mind for them and we can see from the previously quoted verse 4 of this chapter of Exodus what that was.

Here we read that God directs Moses to have the people go out and gather a certain amount everyday, whatever they have need of, and God's purpose in this divine directive is, He says, "That, I might prove them." That is, God wants it to be pellucidly clear to this people that they are totally, completely and absolutely dependent on Him. Why? As some sort of a childish display of power? No, certainly not. God's purpose in teaching his children that they totally depend on Him is, rather, to lead them to absolute and unconditional trust in Him. Through the daily gathering of the manna in the desert it is demonstrated to the people in the most graphic way just how dependent they are on God. If He decides to withhold their food from them for even a few days they will perish. From this they can see how completely they depend on God, and further they can also see that God's care for them is indefectible. They can see what they might otherwise take for granted—their dependence on God. Then from the fidelity with which God cares for them, they are led to see that they can trust Him in all things. After all, if they depend on Him for the daily necessities of their life, and He never fails them in this, He can surely be trusted in matters of lesser import.

So too does Jesus wish to impart a similar lesson to us when he teaches us to ask our heavenly Father each day for our daily bread. From this prayer we see that we too depend totally on God for the sustenance of our life, and that since God never fails us in this, we can confide the rest, those things of lesser moment, to His care with perfect confidence. But sometimes all of us are very much like children—we need constant reassuring regardless of how well things seem to be going, regardless of how strong our faith seems to be. We may at one moment, flushed with some success, feel that nothing can shake us, but then just the least little setback and we feel that God has deserted us, so fragile is our faith. This is true not only of us but was true even with those closest to Jesus. How many times does Jesus repeat the words, "Why did you doubt, you of little faith?" It seems to be a constant refrain in the New Testament, even at times when the Apostles are outdoing themselves in some titanic act of faith. Thus for example during the night immediately after Jesus had so dramatically demonstrated his power by feeding the five thousand with five loaves and two fishes, and when, it may be supposed, the Apostles' faith was very strong. Even at such a moment we see a very striking example of this mixture of faith of the very strongest sort, side by side with weakness.

After the five thousand had been fed and the crowd dismissed Jesus sent the Apostles on ahead over the Sea of Tiberias by boat while he withdrew to the mountain to pray. After laboring long at the oars against contrary winds late into the night the Apostles think that they see Jesus coming to them, walking over the stormy sea, and they cry out for fear. Jesus wishing to allay their fears, speaks to them saying, "Be of good cheer; it is I; be no afraid" (Matthew 14:27). But Peter apparently wasn't convinced and wanted some further assurance that it really was Jesus, and so he cries out, "Lord, if it be thou, bid me come unto thee on the Water. And he said, come." But imagine the incredible faith of Peter! To believe that Jesus could make him walk on water! Imagine the faith that would be required to step over the side of a boat in the middle of a raging sea and expect to walk on the water! Well, Peter did it, "And when Peter was come down out of the ship, he walked on the water, to go to Jesus." Surely, this must be one of the most powerful demonstrations of faith in the entire New Testament. One wonders what Peter must have felt when he threw his leg over the side of the boat to step into that raging sea, expecting to walk on it. If that isn't faith, it will certainly have to do until something better comes along. And so, by a faith so strong that it seems beyond imagining, Peter walks on the water. But even here, even with a faith this strong, doubts can arise. He takes his eyes from the face of Jesus and looks at the difficulty involved, and he loses faith. "But when he saw the wind boisterous, he was afraid and beginning to sink, he cried, saying, Lord, save me. And immediately Jesus stretched forth his hand, and caught him, and said unto him, O thou of little faith, wherefore didst thou doubt?" (Matthew 14:30-31) . Thus we see a mysterious mixture of faith and doubt. We see also that even where there is a faith so strong that it can give one the confidence to step over the side of a boat into a storm tossed sea expecting to walk on it, that it is possible, by paying too much attention to the obstacles in our path to lose our confidence.

As we go through life each day we're very much like St. Peter being sustained as he was walking on the water. Each moment of our life, although it may not seem as dramatic as walking on water, requires even more fundamentally that God sustains us lest we sink back into the bottomless sea of non-being. In the prayer which Jesus taught us in which we ask God to give us each day our daily bread our attention is called to the fact of this radical dependence on God our Father.

When we realize how totally dependent on God we are, and how perfectly He has cared for us all of our lives, our faith is enkindled so that we see that we can trust all things to God's care with perfect confidence. Since this is the case, it would make no more sense for us to worry or be anxious about the future than for the lilies of the field to do so.

4 | Let That Mind Be In You Which Was Also In Christ Jesus...

Philippians 2:5

St. Paul in his letter to the Philippians, chapter two, verse five exhorts us to, "Let that mind be in you which was also in Christ Jesus." But what is this Christ-mind that Paul would have us have? What sort of perspective of life did Jesus have? What was Jesus' vision of the world as he walked through it? How did he see things? It would seem that we must know this if we are to be able to follow Paul's command that we are to have "that mind in us which was also in Christ Jesus." In order to gain some insight into the mind of Christ it will be instructive to see how Jesus reacted to some of the situations, events and people that he encountered, as these are described in the pages of the Gospel.

We see the Christ-mind revealed for example in one of the constantly recurring themes in the teaching of Jesus that, "all things are possible to him that believeth" (Mark 9:23). This means that the way in which Jesus looked at the world was in terms of possibilities, rather than in terms of impossibilities. Thus, when confronted with situations that others viewed as hopeless, Jesus saw hope. We read for example in the ninth chapter of St. John's Gospel that Jesus meets a man who has been blind from birth. The friends and neighbors of the man regard his situation as final, impossible to change and hopeless. The man was born blind—obviously bringing sight to such a one is impossible. They assert that, "Since the world began was it not heard that any man opened the eyes of one that was born blind" (John 9:32). Implicit in this assertion is the unshakable conviction that since it never has been done, it cannot be done. So invincible is this conviction that even after Jesus has healed him and he has received his sight, they still regard the cure as such an impossibility that they refuse to believe the testimony of their own senses and claim that this man whom they had known all of their lives, with whom they had played as children, whom they had passed every day and to whom they had given alms, was not the same man but one who merely resembled him (John 9:9). Imagine the power of a negative belief system! If powerful enough, it can actually cause one to refuse to believe the evidence of one's own senses. This cure of the man born blind illustrates graphically the difference in the way in which Jesus looked at this particular life situation, that of blindness, from the way in which his contemporaries did. They look at a man who is born blind and see a situation which is hopeless, one about which nothing can be done. Jesus looks at the same situation quite differently. As he sees it, *if we can believe, all things are possible.* Thus, he asks the blind men in Matthew 9:28-29, "Believe ye that I am able to do this? They said unto him, Yea, Lord. Then touched he their eyes, saying, According to your faith be it unto you."

With faith all things are possible, because through faith a new vision is given to us and sublime new vistas of human potentiality are opened up. Faith, then, enables us to look at life the way Jesus did—in terms of almost limitless possibilities and richness. When Jesus looked at the world and saw people who were blind, lame, deaf, dumb, and crippled, he did not see them as those whose vision is impaired by the spiritual myopia of a faithlessness which regards these situations as final, definitive and hopeless do. Rather as he looks at these people, seeing them from the perspective of the Christ-mind, he sees them as potentially whole again, provided they can believe. Thus when Jesus looks at a man who is lame, even though the infirmity be of 38 years duration (John 5:1-9) he does not see his condition as impossible to change, nor does he see the situation of a blind man or deaf person, or a paralytic as hopeless. And even when we come to what would seem to be the paradigm case of impossibility, that of death, even death itself will be "swallowed up in victory" (I Corinthians 15:54).

We can see this illustrated in a very powerful way in the story of the raising of Lazarus from the dead which occurs in the eleventh chapter of St. John's Gospel. Not only is Lazarus dead we are told but he has been sealed in the tomb for four days and by this time his flesh has putrefied and decayed. Thus, Martha, the sister of Lazarus, says to Jesus, "Lord, by this time he stinketh for he has been dead four days." It is well to note that even Martha, Martha who sees with the eyes of faith—for she says in verse 27, "Yea, Lord: I believe that thou art the Christ, the Son of God . . ."—even Martha cannot see the resurrection of Lazarus as within the realm of the possible. But for Jesus, even death itself is not an impossibility, but with faith can be overcome. Jesus says, therefore, in verse 25, "He that believeth in me, though he were dead, yet shall he live." And so Jesus, ". . . cried with a loud voice, Lazarus, come forth. And he that was dead came forth, bound hand and foot with grave clothes: and his face was bound about with a napkin." But notice that even such an absolutely astounding manifestation of Jesus' power does not produce belief in those who refuse to see. And so John tells us in verse 46 that some of those that were present and had witnessed the raising of Lazarus were so narrowed and hardened in their limitation thinking that rather then accept this victory over death as a possibility, they preferred to reject the manifest evidence of their own eyes and instead went off to the Pharisees so that they might foment a plot to destroy Jesus.

Again, when it came to people, Jesus looked at them from the unique perspective of the Christ-mind. Thus, those whom the contemporary society had written off as worthless, good-for-nothings, irremediably mired in evil—the prostitutes, the hated publicans, who as tax collectors were the local rip-off artists, simple fishermen who were insignificant nobodies in the eye of society—all of these Jesus could look at with the Christ-mind and see in them not persons immutably fixed in hopeless situations, but rather with Christ's vision sees each as a unique, never to be repeated image of God, with potentialities for good that are quasi-limitless in their possibilities for development.

We read, for example, in the 19th Chapter of St.

Luke's Gospel the story of Zacchaeus, chief among the publicans, which is to say, chief among the local thieves who preyed upon the public under the guise of legality as tax collectors. According to Luke, Zacchaeus wished to see Jesus, "who he was" (Luke 19:3), but was prevented both because of the throng of people and because of his short stature. And so he ran ahead and climbed a sycamore tree so that he might catch a glimpse of Jesus. And, Jesus as He was passing by, came to the tree and looked up and spotted Zacchaeus and called out to him, "Zacchaeus, make haste and come down; for today I must abide at thy house" (Luke 19:5). Zacchaeus, of course, scrambled down and received Jesus as his dinner-guest with great joy, and after dinner declared that he would give half of all his possessions to the poor, and restore fourfold to everyone he had wronged. And so, Jesus declares that salvation has come to Zacchaeus, and then we catch a glimpse of what Jesus saw when he looked up in the tree—what he saw, but what no one else apparently could see in this little thief—a true son of Abraham, one who was not irredeemably lost in wickedness, but one whose heart could be opened to the generous love of God and his fellow man. And whereas his talents and energies had before been utilized in a merciless extortion and exploitation of his fellow men, now these same energies would be turned into creative, enriching, God-directed channels of service of his neighbor—"Behold, Lord, the half of my goods I give to the poor." And in the concluding words of Jesus we catch a glimpse of "that mind which was in Christ Jesus" when he says, "For the Son of man is come to seek and to save that which was lost" (Luke 19:10). This is the Christ-mind.

We see this approach of Jesus to people manifested on every page of the Gospels. And so Jesus looks at another tax collector, also a thief and an extortionist, Matthew, and sees not only the evil of avarice which everyone else sees in Matthew, but also a tremendous potentiality for good. Just as the lame or blind man is crippled in his physical body, but capable of cure, so also is this man who is spiritually crippled, capable of being healed, so that he can spiritually arise, and walk in a newness of life (Romans 6:4). When Jesus looks at Matthew he sees not only a dishonest tax collector—He sees a potential apostle who will go on to give his life in service for others.

So, too, with Mary Magdalene, the sinful woman mentioned in the seventh and eighth chapters of Luke, who had given herself up to every manner of sin. She is described as having seven devils, that is a plentitude of wickedness, in chapter 8:2. As Jesus is at table, having been invited to dine with a certain Pharisee, a woman of apparently notorious wickedness approaches him, and we are told, ". . . stood at his feet behind him weeping, and began to wash his feet with tears, and did wipe them with the hairs of her head and kissed his feet, and anointed them with ointment." His host sees in the woman only a harlot, so abandoned to sinfulness that she is beyond hope. But Jesus looks at her and he sees not only the sinfulness, which everyone else sees and which is apparent enough, but he has also discerned her deep interior spiritual beauty— ". . . she has loved much," he tells us (verse 47). He sees a person whose desire to be loved and to love in return has only been misdirected, not corrupted beyond repair. Jesus sees in the woman a heart that is capable of great love, and thus the possibility of a most fruitful and enriching life when it is dedicated to God, in service to Jesus, and to her brothers and sisters in the Lord.

So Jesus' way of looking at life and people was always to see in the person, regardless of how outwardly depraved they might seem, not only the evident wickedness, but also the deep seated, intrinsic goodness. He saw not only the exterior surface, but also the interior workings of the heart, as is said in the First Book of Samuel 16:7—". . . For the Lord seeth not as man seeth; for man looketh on the outward appearance, but the Lord looketh on the heart." So long as the person desires it, redemption, a new life, is always possible; hope is always present. Jesus, as if to give the greatest possible emphasis to this approach of his to persons, demonstrated it to us in a most graphic fashion in the last moments of his life as he is dying on the cross, when he promises one of the thieves, a person who had given over his entire life to crime and is finally paying the price for his wickedness, "Today shalt thou be with me in paradise" (Luke 23:43). It would seem that what Jesus is trying to tell us is that regardless of how hopelessly evil a person seems to be that the spark of divine goodness is never quite completely extinguished; that our life, regardless of how many mistakes we might make and how bad it may seem, even in our own eyes, is never ruined beyond repair. As Jesus sees us, we are always open to the possibility of a divine love that can transform us and change our life so that we might live up to our authentic God-given potentialities.

This, then, is the way that Jesus looked at people, the Christ-mind. It is also to be our approach, if we are to "let that mind be in us which was also in Christ Jesus." This means that if we are to follow the Pauline mandate we are to see people as Jesus did, that is to attempt always to see in others that scintilla of divine goodness, even where the person attempts to obscure it as completely as possible by his vicious actions. And just as Jesus was able, by love and kindness, by sympathy and understanding, to draw forth the goodness, love and generosity of which they were capable from prostitutes, extortionists, thieves and seemingly hopeless social derelicts of every stripe and sort, so also are we called to try to elicit the goodness of which they are capable from those with whom we come in contact by seeing them as Jesus would see them, and treating them with the love and understanding which Jesus brought to every human encounter.

Another very interesting insight into the Christ-mind may be gained from a reflection on the multiplication of the loaves and fishes, recounted by all four evangelists. We are told in St. Mark's Gospel (6:35-44) that the crowd had followed Jesus and that they were in an isolated place, a desert place to use Mark's descriptive, and that the day was far spent and that they had nothing to eat. Jesus takes compassion on their hunger, first of all their spiritual hunger for they are like sheep having no shepherd (verse 34). And after having satisfied their spiritual needs by his teaching, he also wishes to satisfy their physical hunger with food. But what to do? Their own provisions are depleted and besides the crowd is great, five thousand men, not counting women and children. The apostles urge Jesus to dismiss them so that they can go into the neighboring villages and get provisions. But Jesus wishing to lead them little by little into the Christ-mind looks at them and throws down this challenge—*"You* give them to eat" (verse 37). He knows that they have latent God-like powers and potentialities within them that they have not yet dreamed of but which he must educe. The response of the apostles in verse 37 is one of the most interesting exchanges between them and Jesus in the entire New Testament. Quite piqued by Jesus' attitude it would seem, they reply, really rather sarcastically, the equivalent of—"Oh sure, we're going to go into the villages and buy bread to feed well over five thousand people, right?" The actual scriptual text reads: "And they say unto him, shall we go and buy two hundred pennyworth of bread, and give them to eat?" Two hundred pennyworth being, it is estimated, the equivalent of pay for 8 months work, six days a week, which they most certainly did not have. We are told in a parallel place, John 6:6, that Jesus wished to prove them, that is, to see at what level their faith was. They had, after all, just returned from the first mission upon which Jesus had sent them, and they had come back flushed with success—they had worked many miracles, curing the sick and even driving out demons (Mark 6:13, Luke 9:10). For all of this, however, they were not up to a challenge so great as this. So Jesus takes them step by step, leading them forward, in order to show them the possibilities that faith opens up to them—"all things are possible to him that believeth" (Mark 9:23).

In the description of this event which is given in the sixth chapter of John, verses 8 and 9, we see in a dramatic way the difference between the way Jesus looked at the world, that is, the Christ-mind, and the way in which the apostles, and unfortunately probably most of us, look at it. Andrew approaches Jesus and announces, "There is a lad here, which hath five barley loaves, and two small fishes: but what are they among so many?" (verse 9). In this statement of Andrew we can see quite clearly the difference in the way that he, and it is to be feared the way we, also, look at the world. Andrew looks at the five loaves and two fishes and what does he see? Five loaves and two fishes. But when Jesus looks at the five loaves and two fishes, because he sees from the standpoint of the Christ-mind what does he see? Something quite different. When Jesus looks at the five loaves and two fishes, because he thinks from abundance, he sees not merely the five loaves and two fishes which are evident to the physical senses. No Jesus looking from the standpoint of the Christ-mind sees in those five loaves and two fishes enough to feed thousands of people. Andrew, who stands for most of us, does not see with the eyes of faith and therefore sees only the surface, the external, and misses what Plato called the really real, the interior richness hidden behind the surface, which only faith reveals. And because Andrew's vision is so impaired, he thinks from limitation rather than abundance. Jesus, on the other hand, seeing things from a divine perspective, sees limitless possibilities. Without faith, one looks at the world and sees only one dimension, the material, the surface. This dimension, to be sure, is real enough, but thinking which limits itself to this alone is flat, one dimensional and needlessly impoverished. It ends by seeing the world only in terms of limitation. Jesus, on the other hand, wishes, by faith, to elevate us to see the world, people, situations and events from the divine standpoint, that is from the standpoint of a super-abundant richness. That is to say, from the perspective of the Christ-mind.

It is not surprising, then, that Jesus can declare in clear and unequivocal terms that his whole purpose in coming into the world is not only that we might have life, which we have in any case, but that we might have *abundant* life. He states in St. John's Gospel 10:10, "I am come that they might have life, and that they might have it more abundantly." And in what will this abundant life consist? From Jesus' point of view, it will mean all things are possible if we can but believe (Mark 9:23). Faith will be the key in this approach to life, and it is faith which will open up new and unhoped for horizons to us. Through faith, there is now hope where before there was no hope, possibilities where there were only impossibilities, richness and abundance, where before there was only poverty and limitation. This is true because when by faith we put on the Christ-mind, we see the world as Jesus sees it, in terms of unlimited possibilities, and abundance, for this was Jesus' purpose in coming—that we might not only have life, but have it more abundantly. And so we can see that Jesus in all of the situations which we have considered, whether they concern persons physically blind, or dead, or spiritually crippled through greed, thieving, or prostitution, or when looking at the earth's substance, thought from abundance, not limitation. Thus when John the Baptist who was in prison heard of the marvelous works and teaching of Jesus he sent his disciples to ask Jesus if he was the one who was to come. Jesus, in reply, tells John's disciples that certain things are happening— "The blind receive their sight, and the lame walk, the lepers are cleansed, and the deaf hear, the dead are raised up, and the poor have the gospel preached to them" (Matthew 11:5). John, of course, knew that the messianic age would be characterized by, among other things, a richness, an abundance, and it is just this abundance that Jesus points to. And all of these things are possible because Jesus looks at the world in an entirely new way, in a way in which it has never been seen before—from the standpoint of abundance.

The radicalness of this revolutionary new approach to life which Jesus proposes may be seen especially in the fifth chapter of St. Matthew. If we are to put on the Christ-mind, to see life as Jesus would have us, that is, to see it from the standpoint of abundance, we must change our whole way of thinking. In order to drive this point home as forcefully as possible, Jesus repeats time after time in this fifth chapter of Matthew—"you have heard it said of old . . . but I say unto you." This means that we must leave aside our old, rigid, inflexible ways of thought, thought patterns which saw things only in terms of impossibilities and limitations and be ready to open our mind to a new way of thinking, a new way of life which will inevitably follow from it, which Jesus came to give to us—which is to say the Christ-mind and abundant life. And what a tremendous breakthrough this new philosophy of life of Jesus is! To see the truth of this claim, we have only to compare it to the usual stereotype categories with which we conceive our daily lives. Helplessly, hopelessly, impotently, we simply accept as inevitable so many conditions in our lives not only that we find unpleasant and distasteful, but also conditions which should be changed. We accept as inevitable the inflationary spiral which destroys our savings and erodes the buying power of our earnings. We see ourselves locked into jobs that we find unpleasant and unfulfilling; we find ourselves day after day, week after week, year after year, suffering the same frustrations as we are stalled in the exact same unmoving traffic jams; we accept it as a given fact that more than 1,600 people will be murdered, more than 96,000 cars stolen, more than 3,600 women raped in one city alone, New York, each year, and we simply passively tolerate this as the inevitable conditions of modern urban life. How really incredibly sterile and uncreative our thinking is, how hopelessly limited! But, of course, these problems, and the myriad of other ones which are crying out for solutions, will yield to creative thinking which does not take as its starting point that the problems confronting us are ineluctable and insoluble.

We can see immediately, of course, that the attitude which is so prevalent in our society today, the attitude which simply accepts these conditions with bovine passivity, stands at antipodes to the way in which Jesus approached life, an approach which accepts nothing as an impossibility, be it physical blindness, deafness, or lameness, or seemingly incurable spiritual sicknesses such as prostitution, greed, or double dealing by public officials, or indeed death itself, the most final and most impossible of all. The Christ-mind, if it is nothing else, is an attitude of hope and optimism. Not a mindless, pollyanna optimism to be sure, but one which is rooted in the sure and simple truth that God loves us and means our good. When we are convinced of this our fundamental attitude toward life must change, for we shall then no longer see ourselves in a hostile world, the helpless playthings of a cruel and sinister fate over which we have no control. No, as Jesus sees it, and as he would like us to see it, *all* things are possible, if we can believe. We don't just have to submit to a world in which so many things are not working as they ought to. We seem, unfortunately, all too frequently to be convinced that we must. So in speaking about prostitution, for example, we say, "it's the oldest profession in the world," meaning thereby, of course, that since its been around a long while, it will be around for a long time to come, and we must simply accept it. Jesus, of course, had a different way of thinking, as we have seen. We are told by our physicists and our politicians that we live in a universe governed by the law of entropy—that is, that the universe is like a giant clock that was wound up at the beginning of creation and has been unwinding ever since, until one day, in the not too distant future, it will have run out of energy and will stop. Jesus, of course, did not look at the universe in this way either. Rather, Jesus with the Christ-mind, could look at five little loaves and a couple of fishes and see enough nutritional energy to feed thousands. When we view things from abundance instead of seeing ourselves as living in a universe in which less and less energy is available until that day in which we shall all be forever interred in the silent glacial coldness of cosmic death, we see the almost unbelievable richness of divine abundance. Instead of constantly being told about how little energy there is left in our world, of how our oil fields will soon be depleted, of how our fossil fuels are reaching the point of exhaustion, why doesn't someone take the trouble to point out to us the almost limitless abundance of energy we have if only we change the way in which we think about it. Why is it that we are not told, for example, that within one person alone there is a potential atomic energy of eleven million kilowat hours, which means that within one individual alone there is enough potential electrical energy to light up the entire United States of America for one week. When was the last time you heard a physicist or politician discourse on that piece of interesting information? If we see the unbelievable energy which is locked up within the atom and which manifests itself in an atomic explosion, why is it that we cannot see the almost limitless potential that this could have to serve our needs in a more humane way?

The reason for this is clear—we have habituated ourselves to thinking from limitation rather than from abundance. And so it is as with all of our problems whether they be inflation, crime, our job, international relations, prostitution, energy or whatever—we do not have to just sit back and supinely accept the inevitability of our fate. Rather, if we think creatively, from abundance rather than from limitation, these problems will yield solutions. As Albert Szent-Gyorgyi has said so well, "Discovery consists in seeing what everybody else has seen, and thinking what nobody else has thought." When we let that mind be in us which was also in Christ Jesus, we see that all things are possible, whether it be that the blind can be made to see, the deaf to hear, the lame to walk, or even the dead be returned to life—and this is the gospel, the good news that Jesus came to declare to us who are sometimes so poor in spirit, that is limited in the way in which we look at life, which is so really abundantly rich with divine goodness, if looked at with the Christ-mind.

5 | Lord, That I Might See...

Mark 10:51

St. Mark, in the tenth chapter of his Gospel, relates the story of the blind man Bartimaeus. We are told that Jesus was passing through Jericho and a great crowd of people accompanied him, when suddenly a blind man, Bartimaeus by name, who had been sitting by the side of the road begging, having been informed that it was Jesus who was passing by, began to cry out loudly, "Jesus, Son of David, have mercy on me." His companion beggars and those who were near him tried to silence him, lest he, an insignificant blind beggar, bother this great and famous prophet, Jesus. But Bartimaeus would not be dissuaded—he wasn't going to let an opportunity like this pass him by! He had heard of Jesus and the great miracles he was able to perform. Perhaps if somehow he could get Jesus' attention, Jesus might take pity on him and cure his blindness. After all, he had done so many other marvelous works—he had made lame men walk, given hearing to the deaf and speech to the dumb. He had even raised people from the dead. Thought Bartimaeus to himself, "what's blindness to someone who can raise people from the dead? Maybe today is my lucky day!" Well, since he was blind and couldn't tell where Jesus was, he decided to use what powers he did have, his voice. So he refused to be silent but cried out all the louder to Jesus. Finally above all of the noise and bustle of the crowd Jesus heard him from some place in the throng and stopped and called for him to come to him. When Bartimaeus had been led up to Jesus, Jesus asked him, "What wilt thou that I should do unto thee?" To which Bartimaeus responded with the request for that which was dearest to his heart, "Lord that I might see." As Jesus looked at him his heart was moved with pity for the man's years of suffering in the unending darkness of blindness, and he healed him, saying as he did so, "Thy faith hath made thee whole" (Mark 10:46-52).

Clearly, one of the most important lessons to be gained from this story is the importance of faith. Jesus states that it is Bartimaeus' faith which has brought him sight. It is faith which gives not only Bartimaeus, but us as well, true vision, not only sight, but much more importantly *in-sight*. In an age which is characterized by such pervasive materialism, and its epistemological and moral corrollaries, skepticism and pessimism, there are few teachings that are more important than an insistence on the necessity of faith. In our age of skepticism we are accustomed to say, and to take it for granted as true, "seeing is believing." As a matter of fact, it is the exact opposite of this which is true. It is believing, faith, which alone allows us to really see.

It is well to note that even in the natural order, that is, on the level of natural faith or belief systems, belief is crucially important in structuring our perception itself. This has been abundantly demonstrated by the work of the twentieth century phenomenologists, and in particular by Maurice Merleau-Ponty in his well known work *The Phenomenology of Perception*. What the phenomenologists have shown is that what we see is really in function of what we *believe* to be the case. In fact, the whole task of much of the methodology of phenomenology is to attempt to strip away the obscuring layered encrustations with which belief systems have covered over and hidden the objects of our perception in order to get to the "things themselves" (*"Zu den Sachen selbst!"* according to the well known war cry of the early phenomenologists) .

The attitude which finds its expression in the popular saying, "Seeing is believing," and which so accurately reflects the approach to life of so many people today is then, really a very naive one. The element which is crucially important is not so much "seeing" (that is, perception) . Rather, the "seeing" itself is conditioned by what we believe. Belief systems, therefore, play an extremely important role in our daily lives. Man, willy-nilly, is a creature of belief. These beliefs, however, are not necessarily positive. He may also be the prisoner of negative belief systems which then function to block him from achieving what he is really capable of. There is a solid grain of truth embedded in the old maxim, "Whether you think you can, or you can't—you're right." That is, belief may play a very positive role in our life in which it allows us to "plug into," so to say, the divine powerhouse of the Christ-mind. In which case, our human potential is opened out onto almost limitless horizons. The theme of such a person's life becomes, as it was for Paul, "I can do *all things* through Christ which strengtheneth me"

(Philippians 4:13).

On the other hand, belief systems can also be self-limiting in which case we are imprisoned within the limited perspectives of what we believe to be the case. Scripturally, this is expressed in a very powerful way in the Old Testament in the Book of Job, where Job says, "For the thing which I greatly feared, is come upon me" (Job 3:2). The fear itself seems to have the power to produce that which is feared. This is also what Emerson a long time ago called a self-fulfilling prophecy. Or, as Blaise Pascal observed, "L'idée d'une chute, détermine l'chute." That is merely entertaining the idea of the possibility of failure in the mind is the surest way to bring it about. If, for example, one is inexperienced in public speaking and one has to make a speech, and after having rehearsed it, one is convinced that he will be extremely nervous, his voice will quaver, and he will end by making a mess of it and forgetting his lines, almost certainly he will. Psychologists tell us that the procedure which he is following is exactly the opposite of the one which he ought to. That is, to achieve a goal, it is only necessary to establish in our mind clearly and specifically what the goal is, and then to desire that goal with "passionate inwardness," to use Kierkegaard's celebrated expression. When we worry, we put this psychological law into operation, but we put it into operation in the exact opposite way from the way in which it is intended to function. To illustrate—a person who worries has a quite specific thing in mind. Further, worry is not just a cool detached intellectual judgment which calculates what the odds are that such and such an event might in fact transpire. Far from it. The object of our worry is seen clearly, and with considerable emotion—fear and dread. This, of course, is to stand the laws of psychology on their head. These laws show that if we desire a reasonable goal, it can be achieved, if only we make it specific, and hold it fast with a burning desire. Worry does exactly this, but to produce a most unwanted result.

A simple illustration will show the truth of this. If I take a board which is, let us say, a foot and a half wide and perhaps a hundred feet long and someone bets me ten dollars that I can't walk the length of it, I will most probably walk the length of it without the slightest difficulty and take my ten dollars. If, on the other hand, we take the same board and stretch it between the towers of New York's World Trade Center and someone bets me $50,000 that I can't walk it, everything is changed. But what has changed? Has the width of the board been made smaller? Has its length been increased? No, quite obviously what has changed is my mind. As Pascal so rightly said, the idea of the fall, makes the fall inevitable. Or as the Scripture has it, "The thing which I greatly feared is come upon me."

From this it seems clear that faith even on the natural level, is a most efficacious force, and can be productive of much mischief if it results in negative, self-limiting belief systems. If the belief-systems are negative and self-limiting they will hold us prisoners within bounds that in no way represent our true abilities. Such beliefs are as varied as the maladies and needless pains and sufferings to which mankind is subject. It might be ill-health—a person believes he is weak and sickly and incapable of robust, vibrant health. It might be with respect to our personality—someone believes she lacks in social graces, in charm, in poise, and has the personality of a "wallflower." It might be with respect to intellectual ability. One believes that with his abilities the only thing he is capable of is being a gas station attendant. Or, it might be any one of a thousand different things. In all of these situations it is not the objective reality of health, of personality, of intellectual ability, or whatever which limits one. It is what one believes about oneself that limits, or, looked at positively, that makes a practically unlimited development possible. So the axiom is still true, "Whether we believe we can, or we can't—we're right."

The reason that Columbus, for example, could discover the "New World" while for ages uncounted before him this had not been possible, was not because of a lack of technological expertise, that the ships available could not withstand such a long and arduous voyage, etc. No, as a matter of fact, Thor Heyerdahl has demonstrated that you can cross the Atlantic, or the Pacific for that matter, on a raft without even taking any provisions, but living from the sea with your bare hands. And one thing else—the human mind. So the problem before Columbus was not that the ships were too limited for such a voyage. It was the thinking of man that was too limited. It believed only what it could see. What anyone could see with his physical eyes was obvious enough. You can see as far as the horizon, and as far as the horizon the world is flat. But Columbus, with eyes strengthened by faith, at least a natural faith, could see what physical sight alone could not see. The reason that Columbus, and no one else before him, could discover a "New World" is because he had conceived of a *new way of thinking* about the world. He had managed to break out of the way of thinking about the world which was the result of believing to be true only that which physical sight revealed. He was able to break out of such a limiting belief-system and think of the world in a new way—the world as round. Once one puts aside the preconceived notion that reality is limited to what one can see and was willing to think of the world in an entirely new way, i.e., as *round,* why then the rest was easy, and Columbus really did discover a *New World.*

The lesson to be gained here should be quite clear —we oughtn't to take the limits of our thoughts to be the limits of reality. But the great inventors and discoverers from the beginning of time have always had to struggle against those who cannot make this distinction. Marconi provides a case in point. One cannot but be in awe of the magnificence of Marconi's conception. He believed that somehow it was possible to break out of the limitations to which we thought the human voice was subject. But imagine, to look up into the air and think—somehow, someway, it is possible to send the human voice around the world, without wires, on thin air! Such was the unlimited thinking of Marconi. It goes without saying of course that when Marconi spoke of his new, less limited way of thinking about the human voice and its possibilities to his friends that they all thought he was crazy. Well, there certainly is no surprise in that. Such has been the reception which practically all new, breakthrough ideas have gotten in the course of human history since time immemorial, whenever someone dares to challenge the limited received orthodoxy. But what is surprising in the story of Marconi is that *after Marconi had succeeded, after he had actually sent the messages without wires,* his friends threw him into the insane asylum. He had done what had never been done before . . . and therefore couldn't be done. Therefore he must be crazy. Such is the power of belief systems in limiting, in enchaining the human potential.

One of the things that is very striking about this event in Marconi's life is its similarity to the story of the man born blind that Jesus cured which is described by St. John and which we considered earlier (John 9:1-38). John tells us after Jesus had actually healed the man, a man that his neighbors had been born and brought up with, they refused to believe their own eyes, but preferred to believe what their pre-conceived belief system dictated. "Why it has never been heard of from the beginning of the world that anyone has opened the eyes of one born blind" (John 9:32). And, therefore, it can't be done. Here again we see the power of a negative, limiting belief system. Because it had never been done, it can't be done. Therefore, they look the man full in the face whom they have known all of their lives and state without embarrassment, "No, it's not him." Concession—"But he does look something like him" (9:8-9).

From all of this it seems quite clear that when it is stated as a fact beyond dispute that, "Seeing is believing," we are dealing with, to put it mildly, a quite naive and uncritical attitude, and one, we should like to suggest, which severely and needlessly limits our authentic human capacities. Such an approach just doesn't do justice to the full range of human possibilities. As we have seen, man is a creature of faith. There is no such option open to man as, you may believe or not believe, as you wish. Man *must* believe. He is a belief structured being. His option is not whether he believes or not. His only option is what he chooses to believe. We have seen on the natural level the tragically limiting consequences negative belief systems can have. We have also seen the tremendously liberating effects that positive belief systems can have, opening up whole new and undreamt of worlds to us, as they did in the case of a Columbus or a Marconi, an Edison, an Einstein, or indeed any of our great men of vision who are capable of seeing beyond what is revealed to physical sight with the power of faith.

Now while it is true that even on the natural level positive belief can marvelously enlarge the range of human possibilities, when we move into the super-natural realm these possibilities are not just increased, but become in a certain way limitless. This is why the Psalmist, in reflecting on the potentialities of man, could say, "you are gods" (Psalm 82:6), so great are our potentialities. Now the way in which we are able to tap the sources of this God-like abundance is through faith. It is by faith that we complete the connection with the divine powerhouse. Jesus, of course, understood this and it is for this reason that he insists over and over again in his teaching "If thou canst believe, *all things are possible to him that be-lieveth*" (Mark 9:23). But in order to tap into the limitless reservoir of divine power we must have faith, we must believe. It is for this reason that we wish to make the prayer of the blind Bartimaeus our prayer, "Lord, that I might see." But to *really* see, not just see in the sense of physical sight, but to see with the eyes of faith; to see the way Jesus saw. It is this type of seeing that faith makes possible. It allows us to see, that is look at the world as Jesus saw it, in other words to put on the Chrst-mind.

When we see the world the way Jesus saw it, what a transformation takes place in our thinking! We no longer look at the world in terms of insoluable prob-lems, limitation, impossibility, desperation, hopeless-ness, as is so often the case today. Because we live in an age which has rejected faith, we have inherited its inevitable legacy—pessimism. We have only to look at the way our thinking is reflected in our every day speech to see this. Don't we say, "It's too good to last;" "You can't fight city hall"; "If it isn't one thing it's another," and so on, and so on, and so on. The litany is endless. Our modern mind-set is epitomized just perfectly by what we take to be the unalterable law which governs our lives—the infamous Murphy's law —"Everything is more difficult than you think; everything takes more time than you think; if anything can go wrong, it will go wrong, and at the worst possible time." What an absolutely perfect, and perfcetly astounding, revelation of the mind of contemporary man! Finally, if some good, by some accident or miracle, should happen to us, what do we say? "Knock on wood," because surely there is some malevolent presence lurking nearby which will quickly correct this momentary slip up and snatch our good fortune from us. Or if by some quirk of fate we should somehow find love, Cole Porter in his well known song, *It Was Just One of Those Things,* probably expresses pretty accurately the feelings of a good many people on this point when the lyricist writes, "our love affair was too hot not to cool down." It's just too good to last. Everything, love included, that is any good has a built-in self-destruct mechanism. The pessimistic lack of faith of which this is the product cuts man off from one of the most beautiful of his authentic possibilities—human growth through what Gabriel Marcel has called creative fidelity in love. The words of the poet Robert Browning which are based on faith, at least human faith, express a much richer possibility which is open to man through the relationship of love when he writes to his beloved Elizabeth, "Grow old along with me, *the best is yet to be!*" An age without faith must, of necessity, see everything and everyone, including oneself, as having the hidden time bomb of death ticking away inside.

Jesus, on the contrary, looked at life in an entirely different way, a much more joy filled and optimistic way. And so shall we if we get to really see. Jesus, therefore, would heartily agree with Browning. Yes, this is the true way of conceiving of the human possibility of a fulfilling love—that life is an opening out, an expanding experience. For the atheistic materialist without faith, certainly, life has a built in self-destruct mechanism, the clock is ticking away, we're all, regardless of age, looking down the barrel of the gun. It's only a question of the length of the barrel. Jesus, had a different way of seeing things. He claimed that if we could have faith, if we could believe in him, even though we were dead, we would live. He minces no words, when he says in the clearest terms possible, "I am the resurrection, and the life: he that believeth in me, though he were dead, yet shall he live: and he who liveth and believeth in me shall never die." (John 11: 25) . And then to show that this was not just an empty claim and that indeed he could in fact back it up, he proceeded to raise a man from the dead, and not just one who was dead, but one who was in a state of putrefaction.

When, therefore, we see as Jesus did with the eyes

of faith, we see things from a resurrectional perspective; life is seen as an expanding experience. It is not seen as an expanding experience. It is not seen as it is depicted in the well known French saying, "Partir, c'est mourir, un peu," "To part, that's to die a little." On the contrary, when life is seen from the resurrectional perspective it is not viewed as a series of doors slamming shut forever behind us, but rather as an opening out, an expanding experience. By faith Jesus wants to teach us a new way to look at the world, a way in which we see ourselves not as petty little insignificant blobs of protoplasm. Jesus wants to revolutionize our thinking. We are accustomed to say with helpless resignation to the inevitable, "Well, nothing's perfect." Jesus says just the opposite. We have God-like powers within us, we are made only a little lower than angels (Psalm 8:5). Therefore, Jesus says, "Be ye therefore *perfect,* even as your heavenly Father which is in heaven is perfect" (Matthew 5:48). That is, we have God-like powers within us, if we only knew it. Faith will allows us to establish the connection with the unlimited source of all power in the universe, God, and will allow us to see ourselves as we could be, and to unleash the tremendous capacities that we have. After all, it only is in relatively recent times, a little more than thirty years ago in fact, that man had any inkling of the incredible power that is locked inside of the smallest speck of matter. When scientists began to think about the universe and the matter of which it is constituted in a new way, it was possible to release the incredible energy which was locked up in even the tiniest speck of matter.

Well, what of man? What is he capable of? If matter has such almost limitless power, are we to suppose that man is capable of less? Assuredly not. But man bereft of faith, sells himself much too short. And it is this narrowness of vision which Jesus is trying to correct in man. When he says in Matthew, "For verily I say unto you, If ye have faith as of a grain of mustard seed, ye shall say unto this mountain, Remove hence to yonder place, and it shall remove; and *nothing shall be impossible unto you*" (Matthew 17:20), he is trying to give us some inkling of the power which is available to us if we will only use it. The teaching which Jesus gives to us is capable of giving us a whole new way of looking at our lives, and the almost limitless possibilities that are open to us through faith. We have only to ask. After all, Jesus has promised us, "Ask and it shall be given you; seek, and ye shall find; knock and it shall be opened unto you" (Matthew 7:7). Our problem seems to be that we just can't believe that God could be that good, that he would give us such powers in Christ. The difference between the saints, who performed uncounted miracles throughout the ages, and who perform them just as certainly today, is they take Jesus up on what he says. They really believe, as one of the great saints, Paul, did that, "I can do *all things* in Christ which strengtheneth me" (Philippians 4:13). Not just *some things*, not just the *easy things*. They really believe that they can do *all things* in Christ who is the source of power and strength. And fortified with this faith they proceed to do them, whether it be a Paul in the first century, a Benedict in the fifth, a Francis in the thirteenth, or any of the countless unsung men and women of faith throughout the centuries, and in our own days who have believed and experienced in their lives the divine power that faith releases. Their faith has enabled them to really see the world and themselves as Jesus does, that is, as open to the most wondrous possibilities. Should we wish also to see in this way we might say with Bartimaeus, "Lord, that I might see . . . *really see.*"

6 | *The Light of the Body Is the Eye*...

Matthew 6:22

There is a famous old couplet which runs,

"And what thou seest too become thou must,
God, if thou seest God, dust of thou seest dust."

The ancient wisdom which is expressed in these lines points out that the way in which we look at life, what we see, plays a determining role in what we get out of life, what we become. It further stresses that the goals upon which we set our hearts seem to have the power to transform our lives. If our eyes are set on God, the infinite source of beauty, goodness, truth and justice, we ourselves shall be transformed in the image of these God-like qualities—"God if thou seest God." Or, if we set our hearts on ignoble goals, ones which do not do full justice to us as human persons created for a transcendent destiny, then too we shall begin to be changed into these baser things—"Dust if thou seest dust."

Jesus, of course, a long time before the above lines were written, saw the importance of the fundamental position which we take toward life. He also saw clearly that the goals which we set for ourselves, if we really desire them, will be achieved. They somehow seem to have the power to pull us toward them when they are set in our hearts with burning desire. Jesus expressed this idea midway through the Sermon on the Mount when he said, "The light of the body is the eye: if therefore thine eye be single, thy whole body shall be full of light. But if thine eye be evil, thy whole body shall be full of darkness" (Matthew 6:22-23) . Through this metaphor of physical sight Jesus teaches us that the basic attitudinal position which we take toward life will be crucially important in determining whether we achieve human happiness or not. In the physical order, for example, the person with sound vision, after he has set for himself some goal, let us say to walk to the movie theatre to see a film, using his power of sight, crosses the necessary streets, stops for red lights and negotiates whatever minor problems such a walk would entail, and finally arrives at his desired goal, the theatre. He has no trouble with such a walk because, first, he has set his goal; second, the goal is definite, not vague; and third, his good vision leads him along the correct path. The person whose vision is seriously impaired, however, cannot do this. It may be that his poor eyesight will cause him to make a wrong turn which leads him way from his goal; it may be that he will fail to see an approaching automobile and suffer a serious injury; or he may encounter any number of other difficulties. Thus also in life, so Jesus teaches, if our spiritual vision is sound, our whole soul, "Shall be filled with light." On the other hand, if our spiritual vision is impaired, or indeed if we suffer from complete spiritual blindness, our whole soul will be "full of darkness." And if the light, that is the spiritual principles which we utilize to guide us through life are, "Darkness, how great is that darkness (Matthew 6:23) .

In this teaching that the "Light of the body is the eye" Jesus uses a metaphor to get across to us the idea of the decisive importance of our fundamental attitudes toward life. Just as the man with sound vision can set goals for himself and move without difficulty toward their achievement, so also can the person whose basic position towards life is sound move toward the achievement of his happiness. If, however, that basic position leads him to establish goals for himself which debase him, then he is filled with darkness. By this Jesus means that if our fundamental moral attitudes, that is, those principles which guide us in the conduct of our lives are ignoble and perverse, then this is going to lead us to a goal just as surely as the other will, but the destination here will be self-destruction.

Thus Jesus insists that our basic position toward life, our fundamental moral attitudes, play a determinative role in the question of whether or not we will reach that point in the development of our human potential of which we are capable. This basic life position means the way we see ourselves, the way we see life and the way we see our fellow man. Do we see ourselves, life and our fellow man as Jesus would?

First, how do we see ourselves? Do we see ourselves as defeated in life or as victorious. St. Paul, having adopted as his basic life position the Christ-mind, saw himself, the world and his fellow man as Jesus would have. As a consequence, in spite of the fact that he is scourged with whips, beaten with rods, stoned, robbed, shipwrecked and more, he does not see himself as defeated. Far from it. None of these things can daunt him. They merely show his tremendous strength—that he, "Can do all things in Christ which strengtheneth him." Those who oppose him might, as it were, "do their damnest," but they could not overcome him. Far from being overcome by these things Paul emerges not only as a victor but *"More than a victor"* (Romans 8:37), for now he has proved for himself and experienced in his own life that nothing can separate him from the love of Christ—not tribulation, distress, persecution, famine, nakedness, peril, the sword. As he cries out victoriously, "Not death, nor life, nor angels, nor principalities, nor powers, nor things present, nor things to come, nor height, nor depth, nor indeed any creature" (Romans 8:35-39). Thus Paul, having adopted as his fundamental attitude toward life the Christ-mind, sees himself, inspite of the formidable forces arrayed against him, not only as a victor, but more than a victor. This is because he looks at himself, life and his fellow man as Jesus would.

Well, how about ourselves? How do we see ourselves? As "Victors, and more than victors" in life's struggles? Or do we see ourselves as helpless victims, defeated by life? Do we see ourselves as filled with vibrant, buoyant health, or do we drag ourselves out of bed in the morning and shuffle listlessly through the day? Do we see ourselves as confidently moving in the direction of our professional goals, or do we see ourselves as helplessly locked into a job which we dislike and which is a dead end street? Do we see ourselves as impotent victims of our political system which simply must be accepted—"You can't fight city hall"—or do we see ourselves as masters of our own destiny, the powerful and all victorious architects of our future?

If we have adopted Jesus' point of view we know that our basic attitude on these things, and on our whole life is one in which we see, "All things are possible," no situation can cause us to worry or despair. When Jesus' contemporaries looked at the blind, for example, they merely saw people who were blind, and perhaps felt sorry for them. They were blind, and that was the end of that. When they saw people who were deaf, they perhaps saw human sufferings which they pitied, but it stopped there. That was the end of that. When they saw prostitutes, they might feel some compassion for their human degradation, but that was all they could do. That was the end of that. Jesus, however, had a new way of seeing—all things are possible he taught, if you can believe. When he looked at a blind man he did not see his position as hopeless, but saw the possibility of sight. He could look at a prostitute and see a saint. He could look at a hated, thieving tax collector and see an Apostle who would be one of the twelve pillars upon which he would build his Church. Jesus' new way of seeing made all of these seeming impossibilities possible, and Jesus came to teach us to see things as he did, to put on the Christ-mind in which all of these things are possible for us. And not just these but even greater than these, for Jesus said, "He that believeth in me, the works that I do shall he do also; and *greater works than these shall he do*" (John 14:12).

Jesus came, therefore, to teach us a new way to look

at life and also ourselves, in which we see ourselves not as powerless victims, but as shapers of our own destiny. We know that if we would "Put on the Lord Jesus Christ," that is put on the mind of Christ, we should see ourselves as Christ did, as capable of doing all things in Christ, and in addition to this as loved most tenderly. If, therefore, we want to see things as Jesus did we should also ask ourselves how we feel about ourselves. Do we look at ourselves as Jesus did? We know that when Jesus looks at us, he looks with love, and he sees in us capacities for development which are almost limitless. Do we see ourselves this way? Do we love ourselves as we ought to? Sometimes people are not only surprised, but even shocked when they are told that they don't love themselves enough. Why, haven't they been told all of their lives to avoid vices such as egoncentricity, and getting "too high an opinion of themselves?" No doubt they have, and such teachings are not only a total distortion of the teaching of Jesus, but also productive of much mischief. Contemporary psychologists have discovered that the root of so many forms of what is called self-destructive behavior is an insufficient love for self and its corollary, a lack of self-esteem. This lack of self-love and self-esteem is the cause of behavior such as alcoholism, drugs, compulsive eating, compulsive gambling and so on. In these behavior syndromes the person seems to be punishing himself, perhaps by such punishment to expiate some subconscious guilt. Sometimes such self-destructive behavior will form itself into a larger life-pattern which will determine the person's conduct step by step until the final destruction of self is accomplished. In the approach to psychology known as transactional analysis this is the so-called "loser's script." It almost seems as though the person is playing a part in a play, and just as the script for the part is inflexible and calls for unvarying words and actions on the part of the one who is playing the role, so also does the "loser" play a role in the drama of life which seems to be as rigid and predictable. Thus for example the alcoholic's excessive drinking starts by destroying the drinker's health and progresses along fairly predictable lines, e.g., damage to his career, injury to his wife and family, until perhaps its culmination in his own total destruction through loss of his life in a traffic "accident." These stages occur so frequently and are so typical that for the trained psychologist it almost appears as though the person were walking through life reading the script of a play, a fact which did not escape Shakespeare's observant eye. As he remarks in *As You Like It,*

"*All the world's a stage,*
And all the men and women merely players.
They have their exits and their entrances;
And one man in his time plays many parts. . ."

The role which the person assigns to himself in the drama of life is a result of his interior self-image. If this image is the result of interior self-loathing and feelings of unworthiness, the person will see himself as defeated, and assign an appropriate role to himself.

One of the central tasks which the Christian religion

undertakes is to try to overcome this way of seeing oneself. The first problem which is taken up by the Bible in the opening lines of the Book of Genesis concerns this problem of self-image. Thus we read concerning man's origin, "And God said, Let us make man in our image, after our own likeness . . . So God created man in his own image, in the image of God created he him" (Genesis 1:26-27) . Here God is teaching man about himself, what kind of a being he is. He is unique in all creation, not like trees or fish or animals or anything else. He has dominion over all of these things, and regardless of how marvelously they might reflect God's divine beauty, they do not begin to approach the sublime dignity of man. Man alone is the very image of God Himself. The Christian religion, then, right from the beginning understood the depths, and the severity, of the problem of self-image, and attempts to come to grips with it by pointing out to man his exalted dignity. He is not just an animal like the rest, perhaps with a more sophisticated central nervous system. No, he, and he alone, is the image of God Himself.

Having shown man what kind of an image he should have of himself, the Christian religion could then go on and take up the other question which is of central importance to man—the question of self-love and self-appreciation. Reduced to its absolutely simplest terms, Christianity has one purpose, and one purpose only—to demonstrate to man in the clearest and most unmistakable terms that God loves him. The meaning and purpose of the life of Jesus can be summarized in this—God wished to reveal in the life of Jesus how much He loves us and how precious we are. God so loved us that He, in a certain way, even loved us more than He did Jesus His only son, since He sacrificed even Jesus for us. The major point that Christianity attempts to make, then, is that God loves us, that is, that we are lovable, and that just as God loves us we ought also to love ourselves. We need have no fear that our love of ourselves will result in our becoming egotists who make ourselves the center of the universe, around whom all other things revolve, or that we will become "swell-headed," or puffed up with a sense of our own self importance. The truth of the matter is that all of these personality deformities are the result not of too much self-love, but rather not enough. The person who is deeply convinced of his own sense of self-worth, of his own interior dignity and his intrinsic lovableness, does not feel compelled to constantly try to prove this. Such efforts are really the result of an interior insecurity, a lack of conviction of self-worth.

This is why Jesus can say, and very correctly, not only that we are to love our neighbor, but that the way in which we are to love our neighbor is *as ourselves*. Further, psychological studies have shown clearly that if we do not have a healthy self-image and self-love that it is impossible to relate adequately to others. It has been shown that the socio-pathic criminal who is guilty of violent, hostile, antisocial behavior in many cases is simply acting out on the larger social screen his own interior hatred for himself. The qualities of cruelty, viciousness and violence which he sees in himself he projects into others and he does to them first what he supposes they will do to him, if given a chance.

On a much less severe level than the outright sociopath, we find persons who just simply have difficulty in getting along with others. They do not seem to be able to relate to others successfully. They seem to lack warmth, to be sardonic and morose, and in general to be persons that we find unpleasant. These abrasive personal qualities are also the result of the way they see themselves. They do not see themselves as warm, open and friendly. Frequently these persons will complain about how unfriendly people are, that the world in which they live is a "rat race," that people "will do unto you, if you don't do unto them first," and so on. What they fail to realize is that we get back from people exactly what we give out.

There have been any number of experiments done which confirm this. In one of the most famous of these experiments two groups of teachers were briefed by the school principal at the beginning of a new term. The principal told each group of teachers that they would be teaching a group of "unusual" students that year. In one case the principal told the teachers that the students were unusually bright, and in the other that the students were usually slow. But what the teachers did not know was that those teachers who had been told that they were teaching unusually bright students were actually teaching those who were, according to their record, unusually slow, while those teachers who were teaching the students who were unusually gifted were told that they were unusually slow. The teachers who had been told that their students were unusually bright went into their classes and were extraordinarily demanding. They required compositions done with perfect spelling, with literary grace; they assigned mathematical problems of the most complex sort, and so on. When the students complained that they were not up to such Herculean intellectual feats the teachers simply attributed this to a very understandable youthful indolence, and insisted that with their genius-like minds they could handle these difficulties, and greater ones besides. The students were rather amazed at first but then they began to act the part into which they had been cast, saying to themselves very probably something like, "Well, I'm a genius, so I guess I'll just have to solve these problems. It's a lot of work all right, but that's the way it goes with us geniuses!" Which is exactly what they proceeded to do. By the conclusion of the year they were performing at the same level at which the really gifted students would have been, had they been in these classes, while the progress of the unusually bright students had slowed to match the level of expectation of the teachers who thought they were unusually dull. The conclusion seems inescapable— what we get back from people is very largely determined by what we ourselves give out.

When we encounter difficulties in dealing with

people most of us think to ourselves, "I wish I could change that fellow so that he wouldn't be such a "sour-ball," or "I wish I could change that woman so that she wouldn't always be making snide remarks whenever I meet her," and so on. We are all pretty much this way. When we run into problems in dealing with others our solution is always the same—we could solve the problem if only we could change the other person. The real solution to our problems of dealing with other people however is really just the opposite. Instead of trying to change other people, what we should do is try to change ourselves. If we can change ourselves and our attitudes toward others, we will change the response which we evoke from them.

Well, all of this might sound quite complicated, and we might wonder just how we could implement a program which would ameliorate our social relations. Since dealing with other people constitutes such a large portion of human life, and since some psychologists who have devoted considerable time and effort to the study of this matter have found that perhaps as much as 98% of our problems concern our dealings with other people, it is quite obviously a very important matter. It is not surprising, then, that since our dealings with other people are the singly most difficult problem which faces us that Jesus would have something to say on the question. Indeed when Jesus was asked by a certain lawyer, "Master, which is the great commandment in the law? Jesus said unto him, Thou shalt love the Lord thy God with all thy heart, and with all thy soul, and with all thy mind. This is the first and great commandment. And the second is like unto it, Thou shalt love thy Neighbor as thyself. On these two commandments hang all the law and the prophets" (Matthew 22:36-40). In the judgment of Jesus, then, in trying to sort out the relative importance of things, all of the vast and varied teaching of the Old Testament, as well as his own teaching in the New Testament can be very easily summed up. First of all we must love God with all our heart. This, as Jesus tells us, is the great commandment, but the second command is like the first one, that is to say, essential to us, and this second commandment is that we love our neighbor as oursleves. In these two precepts, namely the love of God, and the love of our neighbor as ourselves all of the weight of the law, all of the wisdom of the prophets is contained. The two precepts are, of course, intertwined with one another. In vain would we protest our love of God if this love were not manifested in our love of our neighbor. As St. John says on the interrelatedness of the love of God and neighbor, "But who so hath this world's good, and seeth his brother have need, and shutteth up his bowels of compassion from him, how dwelleth the love of God in him?" (I John 3:17). Clearly, our love for our neighbor will not be some abstract notion, but will evidence itself in quite concrete and tangible ways. Thus Jesus, when he responded to the lawyer's question, "And who is my neighbor" (Luke 10:29), did not talk in terms of ethereal theological abstractions, but in the parable of the good Samaritan which followed, talked quite concretely about how we are to treat a neighbor in need, viz. bind up his wounds, take him to a place of shelter, care for him, and so forth. Jesus summarizes his whole teaching concerning our relations toward our fellow man quite simply, and quite succinctly when he says, "All things whatsoever ye would that men should do to you, do ye even so to them: for this is the law and the prophets" (Matthew 7:12).

As we have seen, Jesus used the metaphor of sight to teach us the importance of our fundamental moral attitudes toward life. He tells us that the eye is the light of the body and that if our eye is sound our whole body will be filled with light. By this he means that our basic attitudes toward life are as much an indispensable source of guidance to us in our quest for happiness in life, as the light of vision is in the physical world. When we see the world, ourselves and our neighbor as Jesus did, our fundamental life position will be such that it will furnish us with a sure and certain guidance in our quest for true and lasting happiness. If this is our basic life position, and if it is according to such principles that we conduct our life, then our whole life will be filled with light.

7 | Be Not Conformed to This World: But Be Ye Transformed By the Renewing of Your Mind

Romans 12:2

In the day to day *Sturm und Drang* of our quotidian existence the pressures generated by earning a living, raising our children, running a home, advancing in one's profession, and so on, frequently tend to be so great that there is the all too real possibility of being completely overpowered by them. The struggle of just coping successfully with the day to day problems exacts so much effort that we cannot get sufficient breathing space to really sit back and take stock of things. Unless we make a special effort there is an imminent danger that we will be washed away in the torrential flow of daily events and become so lost in solving our day to day problems with ad hoc remedies that we lose our fixed mooring, which is in Christ. In other words, that we become "conformed to this world," as Paul puts it when he writes, "Be not conformed to this world: But be ye transformed by the renewing of your mind" (Romans 12:2). By becoming conformed to this world, what St. Paul has in mind is of course, adopting those principles and standards that constitute the contemporary *Weltanshauung,* that is, the approach to life which constitutes the base from which we operate in dealing with the varied events of our daily lives. This is, even if without our being consciously aware of it, to let the "mind of the world" be in us, rather than letting the "mind of Christ" be in us, as Paul has suggested we should. We have already seen, even if in only the briefest of fashions, some glimmering of what the Christ-mind is like, the way Jesus saw things, and we have seen that the way Jesus views things stands in marked contrast to the way in which the "world" does, to use Paul's expression. Jesus makes this point of the radical difference between his way of life and what Paul calls the "world's" approach in an especially forceful manner in the fifth Chapter of St. Matthew's Gospel, which is to say with the opening words of the Sermon on the Mount.

These opening lines of Jesus' discourse contain the eight Beatitudes (Matthew 5:3-12). If one may be permitted to do a bit of violence to etymology, we might say that the Beatitudes are exactly that—*Be-attitudes*. That is to say, fundamental attitudes toward life. Further, that the attitudes which Jesus would have us adopt as our own are positive ones, i.e., "Be" attitudes. Or, put differently, they are attitudes which form an integral part of Jesus' general program—that we might have life, and have it more abundantly. Further, if we look at the etymology of the word "beatitude," this time seriously and without any attempt at word-play, we see that the word is derived from the latin word *beatitudo* which means happiness. In other words in these Eight Beatitudes Jesus wishes to give us eight fundamental attitudes toward life which will help us in achieving happiness.

As we reflect on these Beatitudes we see two things. First, each Beatitude is made up of two parts, e.g., "Blessed are the poor in spirit,' the first part, which contains the attitude which Jesus recommends to us, and the second part, "for theirs is the kingdom of heaven," which contains the fruit which such an attitude will produce in our lives. Further, each of the Beatitudes is a seeming contradiction, for example, when we mourn, this will produce consolation, when we are persecuted, that is an occasion for rejoicing, etc. By this sharp contradiction between the first part of the Beatitude and the second, Jesus wishes to drive home as forcefully as possible, the contradiction between the way of life which he proposed and the conventional wisdom of any age, i.e., what Paul has called the "world" in the above quotation.

Secondly, these Beatitudes form an integral part of the whole of the fifth Chapter of Matthew one of whose tasks is, as we have seen, to highlight the difference between the new way of life which is being proposed by Jesus and what his listeners had been taught. This is seen in the series of couplets which we have already alluded to which read, "Ye have heard that it was said by them of old time. . . But I say unto you. . ." Therefore, throughout this fifth chapter of Matthew we have two different "ways" proposed to us—the way of Jesus and the "way of the world." Again, as we have already seen, the "world" can accept only what it sees, and this leads to a very limited and needlessly impoverished conception of the possibilities of human life. Conventional wisdom dictates that we "give back as good as we get." Jesus says "Love your enemies, bless them that curse you, do good to them that hate you." The "world" says, "make hay while the sun shines." Jesus says that we should learn from the birds who neither sow nor reap nor gather into barns. The "world" says with the Latin poet Horace, "Carpe diem," "seize the day," eat, drink and be merry today for tomorrow we die. Jesus says, happy are those who hunger and thirst, and those who mourn. And so with the many seeming contradictions which run throughout this section of Matthew's Gospel. Conventional wisdom, the "world's" way, seeing only the surface, advocates short term pragmatism as its basic attitude toward life. On the long term, however, this leads to self-destructive revenge, divisive greed, enmity, hatred, suspicion, hostility and the whole host of corrosive attitudes which ineluctably lead both men individually, and nations into misery and despair. When Paul says, "Be not conformed to this world," this is what he means. It is just such a mind, or "world," to which we should avoid being conformed.

We see this mind of the world and conformity to it illustrated by Jesus in the famous parable of the Prodigal Son. In the fifteenth chapter of St. Luke's Gospel Jesus tells the story of a man who has two sons. One day, the younger son demands his inheritance of his father and some days later he sets out for a city, whose night life was apparently much more attractive than his father's farm. After running through all of his inheritance in gambling, booze, women and the other fleshy delights which the metropolis offered, he found himself in such an impecunious condition and times so bad that he was forced to return to the only work he knew, the farm, but this time not as the owner's favorite son, but rather as a swineherd. So great was the famine in the land, that he found himself starving and longing to have the food that he was forced to give to the pigs. Finally, after much suffering, the Gospel tells us "he came to himself" (Luke 15:17). He then decided that rather than perish with hunger he would return to his father's house and beg to be hired as a servant, where he would at least have food enough to keep body and soul together. We are told that after he had arisen from his miserable condition, and as he was journeying home, the father sees him from afar off and is so overjoyed that he runs to him, hugs and kisses him, put a fine garment on him, and instead of acceding to his request to make him a hired servant takes him into the house and celebrates his return with a joyful banquet.

In this parable we see first of all how the young son accepts the mind of the "world" and becomes conformed to it. The wisdom of the "world" says "grab what you can get while the getting's good." And so he does. He demands and receives his inheritance money, and travels to a famous city, "where the action is." The "world's" wisdom says, "Eat, drink and be merry," or, "Gather ye rosebuds while ye may," for, "they are not long, the days of wine and roses." So he follows the counsel of the "world". It does, after all, look like a real "swinging" program. But he quickly discovers that it leads to disenchantment and his fortunes go from bad to worse, until he is reduced to living with pigs and actually envying them their good fortune. Then in verse 17 the Scripture uses an interesting expression. We are told that "he came to himself." In other words, in his pursuit of the evanescent delights of the flesh and in his exclusive preoccupation with self-gratification, he had apparently lost himself. He had sought himself with such single-minded purpose in his pursuit of self-gratification that he had succeeded in losing his true self completely. This loss of his true self had driven him to the extremity of a pig keeper, envious of the pigs. But after "he comes to himself," and formulates the design to return home a transformation quickly takes place. Instead of being a starving swineherd, he becomes the object of his father's love and the guest of honor at a sumptuous meal. By becoming *con*-formed, that is made one with, or formed by, the "world", he became *de*-formed, that is turned into something he really was not meant to be. By being con-formed or shaped by the "world's" axioms for achieving happiness, his true identity was de-formed into a swineherd. When he rejects the "world's" questionable wisdom which has led him to this plight he becomes *trans*-formed from the mud spattered, malodorous, filthy pig keeper back to his true estate. *Con*-formity to the "world" had lead to de-formity. A rejection of this *con*-formity has lead to a *trans*-formation which was accomplished by the "renewing of his mind," i.e., "he came to himself."

St. Paul puts this together very succinctly when he says, "Be not conformed to this world: but be ye transformed by the renewing of your mind" (Romans 12:2). In other words rather than being transformed by the world, we are to transform the world. But before we can transform the world our own minds must be renewed. Because of the ever present danger of being submerged under the flow of daily cares, problems, and responsibilities, our mind must be constantly renewed, and when our mind is renewed we become transfromed, according to Paul. But what will this transformation be like which is accomplished through a renewal, that is a making new again, in us of the Christ-mind, tarnished by the wear and tear of daily events? When we are thus renewed Isaiah tells us, "they that wait upon the Lord shall *renew* their strength: they shall mount up with wings as eagles: they shall run and not be weary: they shall walk and not faint" (Isaiah 40:31). This renewal takes place, of course, especially in prayer, that is in those moments when our mind is in contact with God. When our spirit is in contact with God it is renewed, or made new again, because by this contact we become God-like. That is to say, we lay aside the human pettiness and the limited perspectives within which we are held, and our minds soar, like the eagle in its majestic flight. We think God-like thoughts, the sublime vistas of the divine mind are opened to us. This is why Isaiah can say that we will "mount up on eagle's wings," and further that this soaring flight will "renew our strength," because when our soul takes this much needed flight it is set free from the narrow confines of the vision which the pressures of day to day toil inflicts upon us. The soul, by taking flight in prayer, is able to soar above the trivialities on which we expend ourselves and the banality of some of our daily concerns and regain its perspective on life.

The scripture also says that, "Thy youth is renewed like the eagles'" (Psalm 103:5). But what is there about the eagle that makes it such a favorite symbol in Scripture? Well first of all there is the matter of vision. In our ordinary language usage when someone has a particularly acute sense of sight we frequently call him "eagle-eye." So when we say our youth is renewed like the eagle, this has the sense that we aquire acuity of spiritual vision similar to the eagles'. This means that just as the eagle can soar in lofty flight and still spot its prey from a long distance, so also can we, when our mind has been energized by prayer, rise far above the petty concerns of daily existence, and from the vantage point of this height, discern what is truly important and what is really quite inconsequential. Further, the eagle glides *effortlessly* through the air, sometimes catching an air current and riding it without even the necessity of moving its wings. When the eagle takes flight he is in his element. He gives himself to the wind with the complete confidence that it will sustain him. Similarity, when man's soul is borne aloft in prayer, when man is in contact with God, his soul takes flight. It, too, is in its element and can glide along effortless, sustained by the divine power. Thus strengthened, it can, as Isaiah says, "run and not be weary . . . walk and not grow faint."

When we pray, therefore, we open our soul to God

the source of all beauty, of all goodness, of all truth, and we bathe our souls as it were in these salubrious divine rays. This rejuvenates our soul in the strict etymological sense of the term rejuvenate, that is, it restores our youth. Instead of being forced into a mold of impersonal inauthenticity by society, by this spiritual renewal we are able to break out of the deadening daily routine, and being renewed, to transform society, rather than be transformed by it. To be sure, in order to do this great spiritual reserves are necessary and these spiritual reserves must be constantly renewed if we are not to be "conformed to this world." The way in which this renewal takes place is by putting on the Christ-mind, for when we have done this, this gives us the power to change our lives as individuals and not only our individual lives, but to become that little heaven that Jesus spoke of, which though little, leavened the whole loaf of society.

If, therefore, we can change the interior leaven of our lives, that is our thoughts, and if we can put on the Christ-mind, we can change our lives. The Book of Proverbs says, "For as a man thinketh in his heart, so is he" (Proverbs 23:7). It is our thoughts which make our lives to be what they are. If our minds are filled with dark thoughts of hatred, revenge, jealousy, suspicion and the like this is the way our life will be. If on the other hand we have the Christ-mind in us, if we love our neighbor and attempt to see what is best in everyone as Jesus did, this gives a whole different cast to our thinking and also to our life. There is a well known legend which illustrates this point very well. There was, according to the legend, a certain very rich king who in order to amuse himself decided to hold a contest. The contest was as follows. He sent his servants throughout his kingdom with instructions to find a completely good, kind, truly unselfish man. When they had found such a man who was in every way without fault, filled with good will and kindness toward his fellow man, the king instructed him that he had a year's time during which he might travel wherever he wished in order to search out and find a really mean, vicious, hateful individual, and after he had found him, when he should return with him, he was promised a very rich reward which he might use as he saw fit, for his own amusement, or to feed the hungry, care for the sick, or in whatever way he wished.

He next instructed his servants to go forth into his kingdom and to seek out the most vicious, embittered, meanest man they could find. When they had returned with him, the king instructed him that if, within a year's time, he could return with a man who was truly good and noble, kind and loving toward his fellow man, he should have a very rich prize which he might use in whatever way he should desire—on the gratification of his sensual desires, on debauchery, to revenge himself on his numerous enemies or whatever.

At the end of the year's search, so the legend goes, both men returned unsuccessful. The good man, in spite of his burning desire to gain the rich prize so that he might use it to help those less fortunate than himself, had been unable to find even one man that, in his judgment, was really mean and vicious. The second man, in spite of his greed and an all consuming passion to gain the prize so that he might inflict pain and suffering on his enemies, was also unsuccessful in his quest to find even one man that, in his view, was truly good and kind.

It seems that in life we tend to get pretty much what we are looking for, or as Proverbs has it, "As a man thinketh in his heart, so is he." If the soul, our window on the world, is covered over with greed, suspicion, hatred, envy, then we tend to read these qualities off in other people and this makes for extremely difficult interpersonal relations. If on the other hand our spiritual vision is unobscured by such distorting lenses and we see the world and other people as Jesus did, then we have no such problems. Jesus, as we have seen, could look at a thieving, hated tax collector and see a potential disciple; he could look at a prostitute and see a potential saint; he could look at plain, ordinary fisherman and see Apostles. When we "let that mind be in us which was also in Christ Jesus," then this is the way in which we shall also see the world.

To be sure there are many factors at work in the world in which we pass our daily lives which certainly do not promote a Christ-like vision of the world, and not only do not promote it but stand in outright opposition to it. There is no doubt that there is a very heavy and a very real drag in daily existence which constantly tends to pull us toward an unquestioning and an unresisting acceptance of the conventional wisdom; to simply be submerged in the faceless and impersonal "they-self" as the existentialists call it. This is a mindless acceptance of whatever society happens to dictate at a given moment. This is to be "conformed to this world," as Paul sees it. But if we are to achieve our true human stature, we are not just to be so conformed, but rather, having been transformed ourselves by the renewing of our mind, we are to transform our society according to the vision of Christ rather than be transformed by it into its image.

8 | If God Be For Us, Who Can Be Against Us?

Romans 8:31

There are no doubt times in all of our lives when the tide of human events seems to be running against us, and perhaps even with such vehemence that it would carry us away in its surge. Certainly this was true for St. Paul. In his second letter to the Corinthians 11:23-33 Paul for a moment at least, draws aside the veil which customarily surrounds his personal life and allows us to catch a glimpse of the hardship and sufferings he had endured in working to establish the infant church. Here Paul says of himself, "Of the Jews five times received I forty stripes save one. Thrice was I beaten with rods, once was I stoned, thrice I suffered shipwreck, a night and a day I have been in the deep . . ." (II Corinthians 11:24-25). One cannot, therefore, but marvel at, and be inspired by Paul's paean of triumph in Romans 3:31 which begins with the words, "If God be for us, who can be against us?" One can only imagine the terrible pain which he must experienced as his back was flayed with the whip, his bones broken and crushed from the blows of the rocks. And yet in the midst of all of this, with the thongs of the cruel whip whistling through the air and laying his flesh bare to the bone, with rocks bouncing off his skull, adrift alone on a plank in the middle of the sea, Paul can still cry out, "If God be for us, who can be against us?" Well, in Paul's case at least, at times it must have seemed just about everyone. In fact talking about who was against him, he says he was in danger on all sides, ". . . In perils of robbers, in perils of mine own countrymen, in perils by the heathen, in perils in the city, in perils in the wilderness, in perils in the sea, in perils among false brethren . . ." (II Corinthians 11:26) . So it was not because Paul had trodden a primrose path that he could sanguinely write, "If God be for us, who is against us?" No, quite the contrary. In his own life he had faced danger of every sort, and on every side. But in spite of this, regardless of how redoubtable the forces arrayed against him might appear, they were powerless, for he was armed with, "the shield of faith, . . .the helmet of salvation and the sword of the Spirit . . ." (Ephesians 6:16-17) . If God is for us, as indeed he is, regardless of how insurmountable the obstacles in our path, regardless of how fearsome those opposing us might seem, they are as nothing. Of course, it requires faith to see this. But for God's saints it has been ever thus.

This point, that regardless of how dread the foe or impossible the odds may seem, if God is with us, nothing can prevail against us is illustrated very beautifully in the story of David which is related in First Book of Samuel. We read in Chapter 17 that the Philistines and the armies of the Israelites were drawn up for battle on opposite sides of the valley of Elah. Each day, morning and evening, a great giant of a man, probably about 10 feet tall ("six cubits and a span") , came forth and mocked the Israelites, challenging them to single combat. The size and strength of Goliath were so fear-inspiring that no Israelites could be found who had enough faith that God would see him through the combat to accept the challenge. At the same time David who was still a pink-cheeked young lad was at home tending his father Jesse's flocks when his father called him and directed him to bring provisions to his brothers who were encamped with the armies of Saul at Elah. As David approached the encampment it chanced that Goliath was just then mocking the Israelites for their cowardice. When David learned that there was no one in the entire army of the Israelites with the courage of heart, and the faith in God, to fight the Philistine giant he said to King Saul, "Let no man's heart fail because of him; thy servant will go and fight this Philestine" (I Samuel 17:32) .

But Saul, eager though he was to have the reproach removed from his armies, did not take David seriously and told him that he was too young to take on this experienced warrior. Then David related to Saul some of the things that he had been able to do because God was with him. He tells Saul that while tending his father's sheep at sundry times a lion or a bear would descend on the flock and make off with one of the sheep. At such times, when the spirit of the Lord was on him little David would pursue the lion, catch him by his beard, and tear the prey from his mouth with his bare hands! "And David said unto Saul, thy servant kept his father's sheep, and there came a lion and a bear, and took a lamb out of the flock: and I went out after him, and smote him, and delivered it out of his mouth: and when he arose against me, I caught him by his beard, and smote him and slew him. Thy servant slew both the lion and the bear: and this uncircumcised Philistine shall be as one of them, seeing he hath defied the armies of the living God" (I Samuel 17:34-36). David, armed with nothing else than his faith in God went out after a lion and a bear, and with his bare hands slew both of them, and he asserts to Saul that this Philestine will fare no better against him than the lion or the bear did.

After hearing this rather impressive story of David's prowess, Saul is finally persuaded to let David go forth to meet Goliath in single combat, and so he placed his own armor on David. But after they had David all outfitted with Saul's weighty protective gear, it proves so heavy that David, who is still only a boy cannot lift his legs to move from the spot. Besides, David really doesn't need it in any case, for it will not be by dint of natural means such as superior armor that David will overcome the Philestine champion. It will be because "God is with him." So the armor is removed, and the boy sallies forth to fight the fearsome giant, armed only with his shepherd's staff, five smooth stones which he had taken from the brook, and his sling. As he draws near to Goliath, the giant heaps insults on him, and predicts that in very short order his flesh will be furnishing the evening meal for the local vultures. But David, unarmed as he is, and in spite of the size of this formidable giant, who is experienced in battle, and seemingly invulnerable because of his armor, runs toward him without the slightest hesitation. He realizes that if God is with him, Goliath will be unable to prevail against him. Thus David tells Goliath, "Thou comest to me with a sword, and a spear, and with a shield: but I come to thee in the name of the Lord of hosts . . ." (17:45). And then with a whirring of his sling David buries a stone in Goliath's forehead and cuts off his head with his own sword.

Clearly David understood the same thing that Paul did. If God is with us, nothing can withstand us, nothing can prevail against us. It makes no difference how formidable the foe, or how insuperable the obstacles that stand in our way. If God is for us, nothing can overcome us, no matter how dread the circumstances may seem. It makes no difference if it is a bear or a lion. Or, indeed both of them together. It makes no difference if it is a ten foot giant who is so fearsome that he can single handedly hold an entire army at bay by himself. If God is with even a fledgling youth, he will be victorious.

From this we can see that nothing can withstand the limitless sea of divine power. Further, this infinite divine power is always available to us, provided we can "plug into it." But how do we tap this unlimited source of power which can overcome all obstacles, regardless of how insurmountable they might seem? The answer is found in one word—faith. Would the divine power which overcame Goliath through the boy David not have been every bit as effective if it had operated through Saul, or one of David's brothers, or indeed anyone in the army of the Israelites? Of course it would have. Why was it then that only David could become the conduit through which it flowed? Because only his faith was great enough to allow sufficient power to flow which would be equal to the situation. After all, how many people would have the faith to take on a lion, pull the prey right out of its slavering jaws, grab it by its beard, and kill it with his bare hands? And then finish off the bear for good measure. That requires faith of a quite extraordinarily high order indeed. Or who would go forward without hesitation, armed only with a sling and five stones, to meet a ten foot giant? Again, only one whose faith is so great that he is totally convinced that if God is with him nothing can stand against him, regardless of how fearsome the odds might appear to those whose vision is unaided by faith. But once we are filled with faith then we can tap the infinite reservoir of divine power and allow it to operate in what appears to be impossible situations.

This is what Paul meant when he exclaimed "I can do all things in Christ which strengthen me" (Philippians 4:13). Faith makes all things, even those which according to our ordinary human way of looking at them appear to be impossible, possible. We see this demonstrated in the story of Jairus whose only daughter had died and who besought Jesus to restore her. Jesus tells him, "Fear not: believe only, and she shall be made whole" (Luke 8:50). Jesus tells him in effect that if he can believe *all* things are possible, not just some, but even raising the girl from the dead. To the eyes of those without faith there is nothing so final and irrevocable as death. When a person is dead, that's it. Therefore when Jesus comes to the house and announces that he is going to raise the girl from the dead we are told the mourners who have come to pay their last respects "Laugh him to scorn" (Luke 8:53). For them, this is totally impossible. Because their vision is limited to what their eyes can see, they cannot realize that with faith, the infinite power of God can be brought to bear on this situation and the impossible can become possible. As we read earlier on in Luke, "For with God *nothing* shall be impossible" (Luke 1:37). Faith is the channel which places us in contact with this divine source of power.

This too is why Jesus can make such improbable promises to us concerning prayer. He promises us that *whatsoever we desire* will be given to us through prayer, *if we believe.* In Mark 11:24 he states unequivocally, "What things soever ye desire, when ye pray, believe that ye receive them. and ye shall have them." It is important to note that Jesus doesn't say, "some things"; he doesn't say "spiritual things"; he doesn't say "everything except material things such as automobiles, houses, swimming pools, better jobs, sailboats, and that type of mundane nonsense." Jesus doesn't say anything of the kind. He says, and it is impossible to see how he could say it any clearer, *what things soever ye desire,* which does not exclude a beautiful home, car, job, swimming pool, beach house, or whatever. Whatever it is we desire, if we ask for it in prayer, with an unshakable faith, we shall have it. And lest there be any confusion about it, it is not as though we have one text in which Jesus teaches this.

No, Jesus repeated it over and over again because he realizes that when he tells *anything,* we're going to say, with our usual limited thinking, "Well, yes anything—that is, anything spiritual," or anything "holy," or anything "heavenly." But surely he doesn't mean we could ask for "material" or "base" things, or "worldly" things. He surely wouldn't mean that we could ask for more money so we could move into our dream house, or a nice sailboat, or a new wardrobe, or anything like that, which would be first of all so unworthy of our desires, and secondly, so unworthy of God's notice.

Well, Jesus it seems knew us well enough to understand that as soon as he said something that collided with our limited way of thinking, that rather than change our thinking, we would change his teaching to fit our limited mentality. Thus, the old scholastic philosophers triumph again—"Quidquid recipitur secundum modum recipientis recipitur," "Whatever is received is received according to the mode of the receiver," according to their famous saying. So what we do is take the teaching of Jesus in which he wishes to show us that there are no limits to the possibilities, *if we can believe,* and immediatley start to impose the limitations of our limited way of thinking on it.

Well, Jesus, as we noted above, knew full well that we would play our usual game so he did not just say once in Mark 11:24 "What things soever ye desire, when ye pray, believe that ye shall receive them, and ye shall have them." No, he repeats this same teaching over and over again. Thus he says in Matthew 21:22, "And *all things,* whatsoever ye shall ask in prayer, believing, ye shall receive." Again, in St. John, during the discourse of the Last Supper, which he realizes will be the last opportunity that he will have to recall to the Apostles' minds the most important points in his doctrine, he repeats over and over, at least a half dozen times during this discourse alone, *"Whatsoever* ye ask in my name, I will do it" (14:13) . Again, "If ye shall ask *anything* in my name, I will do it." (14:14) ; "That *whatsoever ye shall* ask of my Father in my name, he may give it you" (14:16) ; "Verily, verily, I say unto you, *whatsoever* ye shall ask the Father in my name, he will give it you" (16:23) .

It seems quite clear, therefore, that it is not just one statement of Jesus that we are dealing with which we might attribute to a desire for rhetorical effect or to hyperbole. No, Jesus tells us over and over *whatever* we ask in prayer, if we can believe, we shall have it. In fact God even challenges us to test Him to see if He will do all this. Thus He says, *"Prove me* now herewith, saith the Lord of hosts, if I will not open to you the windows of heaven, and pour you out a blessing, that there shall not be room enough to receive it" (Malachi 3:10) . God dares us to try this thing called "prayer" to see if it works or no. The words here in the Prophet Malachi almost sound like one of our modern day T.V. commercials—kind of like God saying, "try my plan for thirty days and it must work or you pay nothing." "Prove me," God says. That is, if you ask you must receive; if you seek, you will find what you are looking for; if you knock, it shall be opened to you (Matthew 7:7) . But we should be careful to note that it is not just any sort of asking that God rewards by granting what is requested. Rather, we should note quite carefully what Jesus says: "What things soever ye desire, when ye pray, *believe* that ye shall receive them, and ye shall have them." Jesus says, therefore, that it is not just any prayer which will be efficacious, but only the prayer which proceeds from faith, that is the prayer which is made in which we can see in our mind's eye the object of our prayer as already accomplished. So whatever it is that we desire when we pray, we should visualize it in our mind, see in our imagination that desire as already accomplished. We should confidently expect it to happen and we should believe it will happen.

Well, what if we do all of these things and we do not receive what we want immediately. We pray, and as we pray we see in our mind's eye our desire as already accomplished. We confidently expect it and we believe firmly that it will happen. We see ourselves as having shed 40 lbs., as supervisor of our section, as living in the dream house, as rid of the cigarette habit, or whatever. We expect that it will happen, and we firmly believe it. But it doesn't happen. What then? In such a case Jesus teaches us the necessity of persevering in the prayer. Why should this be necessary? If God is going to give us what we desire, why can't he do it right away and get it over with? Does He get some sort of perverse delight in teasing us, telling us on the one hand to ask for whatever we desire, and then when we take Him up on it not giving it to us?

As we noted, Jesus did not say that we would get anything we asked for. What he said was we would get anything we asked for in faith, *"believing* that ye shall receive them."* Now sometimes the proof of such faith is God's withholding what we desire for a time and not giving it to us immediately. Not, indeed, to get some kind of cruel satisfaction from tantalizing us, but to help us to grow in faith which is really the most precious gift of all, since if we have this, we have the key which opens every one of life's doors. Jesus taught us this in his parable of the unjust judge contained in Luke 18:1-5. He tells us that in a certain city there was an unjust judge who feared neither God nor man. A widow woman came to him seeking redress from some alleged injustice. Since the judge cared nothing for God or man, he dismissed her forthwith. But she was not so easily put off, and she came back the next day, and the day after that and the day after that, until finally the judge decided that refusing to grant her her petition was more trouble to him than it was worth, and with her continual pestering she would end by wearing him out. The judge, therefore, decided in her favor, not because of any lofty motive of desiring to see justice done, but simply so that he could finally be rid of her. And the widow's attitude is one that Jesus recommends to us when we pray. That is to say, when we pray we are to be persistent. We should persevere in our prayer even though it is not granted immediately, because God sometimes uses this deferment of our request in order to build our faith, which is the *sine qua non* for efficacious prayer. And when our faith is strong, when we can look at the world and the persons, events and situations with the eyes of faith we are true followers of Jesus' way, and when we see the world in this way we are led to exclaim as another great follower of Jesus did, "If God be for us who can be against us?" We see that no obstacles, regardless of how seemingly insurmountable, no problems or difficulties, regardless of how formidable, can prevail against us. When we have a deep faith we see that God *is* with us. We also see that if He is with us no problem or difficulty can overwhelm us.

9 | Be Not Afraid ...

Matthew 14:27

Of all the human emotions, fear is without doubt one of the most universal, and at times also one of the most destructive. It is cretainly true that fear has a positive side to it in the psychical structure of man, serving as an "early warning system" for us to help us avert impending dangers that threaten our well-being. If one is in an automobile with a friend who has been drinking excessively and who in a moment of drunken recklessness, decides to pass a car on a blind curve, one no doubt experiences fear, and quite rightly so. Here fear has the positive function of activating the gland system to release the appropriate hormones into the bloodstream so that the threatened person might be energized to action which will insure his survival. There are, therefore, many situations in life such as this in which fear has a very positive function as part of our survival mechanism. But although fear is a necessary and useful part of our survival equipment, it can, and all too frequently does, play a very destructive role in human life. It can, if uncontrolled, become one's dominant attitude toward life. In these cases far from serving the positive God-given function for which it was intended, it becomes an oppressive, and indeed at times an intolerable burden. So great a problem has this negative side of fear become for modern man that its investigation, analysis, and treatment has occupied a major portion of the efforts of twentieth century psychology. This is not of course to say that the problem is unique to the twentieth century. It is already mentioned as a matter of fact on the very opening pages of the Bible, as one of man's first reactions to an unpleasant situation. Because man has done wrong and feels that his conduct has been displeasing, he is afraid. Thus we read at the very beginning of the very first book of the Bible, "And they heard the voice of the Lord God walking in the garden in the cool of the day: and Adam and his wife hid themselves from the presence of the Lord God amongst the trees of the garden. And the Lord called unto him, Where art thou? And he said, I heard thy voice in the garden, *and I was afraid,* because I was naked; and I hid myself" (Genesis 3:8-10). Fear, it would seem therefore, has been around as long as man has. Sometimes, to be sure, it is an appropriate response to a threatening situation and part of man's primative survival mechanism. Without it primitive man probably would have tried to go head to head with lions and tigers, in which case the human species would quickly have become extinct. Now while fear did, and still does, help man to survive in a sometimes hostile environment, it can become excessive, and it can become a response to situations which are seen as threatening by the fearful person, but which in reality are not. Fear can become the all pervasive attitude with which we face life. When this happens, it becomes one of the most virulent forces in human life. It is with fear in this sense that we are here concerned.

Jesus, as we have noted many times, came to give us a comprehensive plan which would engender certain basic attitudes in us with which we could respond to the multifarious and variegated situations in life in such a way as to lead us to happiness. Fear, when it has become excessive and is no longer a rational response to life's events, is one of the most excruciatingly painful of the problems with which man must deal. In our modern society fear is not just one problem among others. One has only to look at the vast outpouring in psychology, philosophy, literature, drama, and theology to see that far from being just another problem that man must cope with today, it well may be the problem *par excellence* of twentieth century man. If we are dealing with a problem whose magnitude is of such proportions, and such pervasiveness in the human condition, it would be unlikely that Jesus, who came to give us a teaching which would provide us with a basic position with which we could confront life, would have nothing at all to say about it.

Jesus did, indeed, on many occasions show his followers how to deal with the problem of fear. The New Testament is replete with instances when Jesus says to his followers, "Be not afraid," "Fear not," and so on. In the fourteenth chapter of Matthew, for example, after the feeding of the five thousand with five loaves and two fishes, Jesus had sent the Apostles on ahead of him across the Sea of Tiberias and they are in a boat laboring against a stormy sea. In the middle of the night Jesus comes to them, walking on the water. When they see Jesus they fear greatly, thinking that they are seeing a ghost. Jesus then addresses these beautiful words to them: "It is I; be not afraid" (Matthew 14:27). These words may serve as a guide to us also as we look out across life's stormy sea and like the Apostles are terrified by what appears to be strange and unnatural apparitions. In all such instances Jesus addresses us still as he did the Apostles with his beautiful words of comfort, "Be not afraid."

As we have noted several times, Jesus came to give us a richer fuller life. His teaching enables us to achieve the full development of our human capacities. Now of the many forces that impede this development, one of the most deleterious is fear. One of the most striking, and baneful effects of fear is to paralyze action. We can see this in Jesus' teaching in the parable of the talents. In Matthew's Gospel Jesus illustrates this paralyzing effect that fear can have on action by telling his followers a story. There were three men and their master called them and confided to their care certain of his possessions. To one he gave five talents, to a second two talents, and to another one talent, which they were to put to use and develop so that the master might receive some return from them when he returned from his journey. Upon his return, he called his servants and the reckoning reveals that the first servant had put his five talents to use, had developed them so that the original deposit which had been entrusted to him had doubled. The second servant had done the same. When he came to the third servant, however, we are told that he did nothing whatever to develop the talent which had been given to him. He had undertaken no activity whatsoever by which his talent would have been developed. The excuse which he attempts to fob off on the master is very revealing. He says, "Lord, I know thee that thou art an hard man, reaping where thou hast not sown, and gathering where thou hast not strawed: And *I was afraid,* and went and hid thy talent in the earth: lo, there thou hast that is thine" (Matthew 25:24-25). The reason which he gives for not developing his talent is as he says, " I was afraid."

The insight which the Bible gives us here is excellent, for this is precisely the effect that fear has on us —it paralyzes action. But since human life is dynamic and not static, the talents which God has given to us, just as those which were confided to the men in the parable, can only be developed by *action.* We will not, and cannot, come to our perfection, develop in our God-intended direction unless we *act.* The man who received five talents knew the character of his master just as well as the man who had received one talent. But he did not perceive himself as an insignificant menial totally at the mercy of a tyrannical master, to be disposed of according to his whim. Nor was the master this sort of person. There is nothing in the story to indicate that the master is a vicious despot who fits the description given by the man who had received one talent. Rather, it seems that the attitude toward life of the man who received one talent is so fearful that his fear has altered his perception of his master. He is so timorous with regard to life in general that when he is confronted with an authority figure he is absolutely terrorized. Fear causes him to demean himself in his own eyes, which at the same time causes the master to assume such terrifying proportions that he feels totally at his mercy. In this situation he becomes so fearful that any useful activity is precluded. Morbid fear seems to have this strange ability to immobilize us so that we debar ourselves from any useful activity. The timorous person withdraws from the enriching and fulfilling experiences of life. He is afraid to meet new people, afraid to try new experiences, afraid to seize opportunities as they present themselves, and instead withdraws into himself. The alcoholic for example is frequently a person who is afflicted with this type of morbid fear. He is afraid of life, feels threatened by it and withdraws into himself. He withdraws into his room, locks the door behind him, takes the phone off the hook, and takes out his "only friend," the bottle, the only thing that he seems not to fear, and drinks until he has anesthetized himself from the painful existence which his fear imposes on him.

This withdrawal from action which fear causes can be seen very clearly in the Scripture. After Jesus had been crucified and buried the disciples were afraid. As Jesus had predicted so accurately, "I will smite the shepherd and the sheep of the flock will be scattered" (Matthew 26:31). After the terrifying events of Good Friday the Apostles were so afraid that they hid themselves and locked the door behind them. St. John tells us, "Then the same day at evening, being the first day of the week, when the doors were shut where the disciples were assembled *for fear of the Jews,* came Jesus and stood in their midst . . ." (John 20:19). Fear causes them to take flight and to withdraw. Somewhat later, after they receive the Holy Spirit, they will no longer be afraid, but will go forth and proclaim Jesus so boldly that all will be amazed. But at this time their fear creates a prison for them. Their own fearful minds have imprisoned them just as effectively as if the Jews had caught them and jailed them. This again illustrates the truth of the saying in the Book of Proverbs 23:7, "As a man thinketh in his heart so is he." The person who has been brought to court, found guilty and sentenced to prison has lost his freedom, he can no longer come and go as he pleases. Fear, as we can see here in the case of the Apostles, can function every bit as effectively as a jail sentence. The Apsotles, because of their fearful minds, are no more free to come and go as they please than criminals who have been sentenced to prison. As they think in their heart, that is exactly the way they are. Their fear causes them to see themselves as being under the power of the Jews, and because this is the way they think, the Jews are able to prevent them from circulating freely and preaching the message of Jesus just as surely as if they had brought them to trial and sentenced them to prison. If fear causes us "to think in our hearts," as Proverbs puts it, that we are weak and powerless, unable to deal effectively with our daily problems, that is exactly how we will be—weak, powerless, impotent.

If on the other hand we see ourselves as invulnerable, unconquerable, invincible in the battle of life, if we believe totally that we can do all things in the Christ who strengthens us, then that is exactly the way we will be—invincible. If we see ourselves as weak, sickly, stupid, inept, ugly, then that is exactly how we will be. But if on the other hand we see ourselves as strong, bubbling over with vibrant health, endowed with sparkling wit, gifted with social graces of charm and poise, as enchantingly beautiful, then that is exactly how we shall be. There is perhaps an unsuspected wisdom in the song from the musical Westside Story in which the heroine whose heart, filled with love, overflows in the song, "I Feel Pretty." And without a doubt so she must be. The scripture, using somewhat different language says exactly the same thing. . . "As a man thinketh in his heart, so is he."

In George Bernard Shaw's play *Pygmalion,* Professor Henry Higgins had taken the dirty, bedraggled, unkempt, lackluster flower girl Eliza Doolittle out of the gutter and has decided that he is going to transform her into a ravishing beauty, poised, elegant, with scintillating wit and charm, and finally pass her off as sprung from the blood royal, an authentic Duchess. But work progresses slowly. It seems he has succeeded in taking the girl from the gutter, but not the gutter from the girl. He realizes that if he is to effectuate the desired transformation his attack must be three-pronged. First of all Eliza must change the way she thinks. Realizing that a reciprocity exists between thinking and acting and that the way we act has resonances in the way we think, she must also change the way she acts. Finally, since thought and the emotions are not always subject to reason's control, and since they are affected by what we say, she must change the way she speaks. He summarizes this tripartite attack thus:

> "*Think* like a duchess,
> *Act* like a duchess,
> *Talk* like a duchess,
> Curbstone English keeps you in the gutter."

We know well enough that what we think affects what we say. What may escape our notice, but which is equally true, is that what we say also affects what we think. Now since it is true that our thoughts control our life, and since our thoughts are affected by what we say, by changing the way we talk about ourselves, we will be changing the way we think about ourselves, and by changing the way we think about ourselves we will be changing ourselves. At least if the scripture is right when it says as a man thinketh he is in his heart, so he is. We should, then, stop using all language about ourselves which denigrates our abilities, or our worth. We should stop saying things about ourselves such as "I'm ugly," or "I'm no good at sports. I'm just naturally clumsy." "I have no musical ability—just a tin ear," and so on. These kinds of things which we say about ourselves tend to generate this same kind of bad self-image, and our self-image will be the most potent force at our disposal if we are to meet life and be victorious.

This point is brought out very effectively in the thirteenth chapter of the *Book of Numbers* in the Old Testament. God had commanded Moses to send scouts into the land of Canaan to reconnoiter it in order to ascertain what type of people inhabited it, whether the soil was fertile and so forth. The scouts went forth and after their expedition they returned carrying the fruits of a very rich land, figs, grapes, pomegranates, and much more, and reported to Moses that it was a land flowing with "milk and honey" (Numbers 13:27). Well, needless to say, when the people saw the lush fruit of the land and heard that it flowed with milk and honey, there was a great stir among them. After having been out in the baren desert for so long, just the sight of the figs and grapes was enough to spur them to action. Apparently, one can grow tired even of heavenly manna after forty years of it! And so they are all for proceeding post haste to Canaan in order to enjoy the abundant life that God had foretold would be theirs in this their Promised Land. But the scouts who had just returned spoke up, "We will not be able to go up against the people; for they are stronger than we are . . . and the people that we saw in it are men of great stature. And there we saw the giants, the sons of Anak, which come of the giants; and we were in our own sight as grasshoppers, and so we were in their sight" (Numbers 13:31-33).

Here we see in a very striking way the manner in which fear acts. First, fear distorts the way they see things; second, because of this distorted way of seeing things obstacles are magnified out of all proportion; third, as a result of the first two steps in this process they are rendered incapable of action, regardless of how desirable the goal to be achieved by the action might be. Notice too that fear is revealed here as being a more potent force in determining conduct than motives such as hunger and thirst, which we usually think of as being much more primordial and much more exigent. Because they are afraid, they see the men as giants. Fear has caused the obstacles to be greatly over exaggerated. The obstacles appear to be so great that their puny powers would be worthless against them. Further, fear causes their perception of themselves to be so completely distorted, that according to their own evaluation of themselves, they are *grasshoppers*. Such is the devastating effect that fear can have on our self-image! Notice, too, that the way they see themselves, is exactly the way others see them, and it will determine precisley the way they are treated. And so we read that not only were they grasshoppers in their own eyes, but that is exactly the way the Canaanites saw them also. "And we were in our own sight as grasshoppers, *and so were we in their sight.*" It goes without saying of course that anyone who sees himself as a grasshopper is not going to deem himself worthy of very much that is worthwhile in life. Here fear has caused them to so undervalue their abilities that action which will bring about a worthwhile goal is impossible.

This power of fear to cause us to misperceive things

is also illustrated by comparing two different events in the life of Peter. Immediately after Christ had been taken prisoner he was being interrogated by the high priest and Peter had followed along at a distance to see the outcome. As he sat by the fire warming himself outside the palace of the high priest, "A damsel came unto him saying, Thou also wast with Jesus of Galilee. But he denied before them all, saying, I know not what thou sayest" (Matthew 26:69-70). Here we have Peter who later on will proclaim Christ so boldly before all, terrorized by a little girl! He is so dominated by fear that a child can control his behavior, even to the extent that he denied that he even knew his own best friend. If we allow fear to govern us even children can control our actions. In Peter's own eyes at this moment he probably saw himself as a little less than a grasshopper, while the little girl loomed over him like one of those legendary ten foot tall sons of Anak. And so she dictates how Peter acts, even to doing that action of all actions that he regards as most abominable.

Here Peter's fear causes him not to see himself as he really is. The image of his true self has been obscured by his fear. Later on, after he receives the Holy Spirit he will remember who he really is and he will see himself truly according to his authentic God-given potentialities. Fear will be shed as a cloak, and the true Peter, with all that he is really capable of, will be revealed. This is clear in the third and fourth chapters of the Acts of the Apostles. Peter and John are going up to the temple at the ninth hour to pray and as they are about to enter the temple a beggar who has been lame from his mother's womb asks them for an alms (Acts 3:1-3) . Peter heals the man and a crowd gathers. Peter, against the strict orders of the high priest and the Sanhedrin, begins boldly to preach the Lord Jesus. As he is preaching the priests, the captain of the temple and the Sadducees lay hold of him and John and throw them into prison. Next day they bring them forth before Annas the high priest and Caiaphas the very ones who had so terrified him before that just being outside of their house had caused him to become so fearful that he allowed a little child to control his behavior, to the extent that he did the most reprehensible thing that he could imagine, i.e., denying his best friend Jesus. But now he is no longer dominated by fear. He doesn't see himself as a grasshopper and these men as giants. Fortified by faith, he sees himself as unconquerable. The high priests and indeed the whole assemble cannot compel him to say what he doesn't want to. Rather, he boldly and fearlessly preaches the forbidden name of Jesus to the high priest and those who had conspired to put Jesus to death. "Be it known unto you all, and to all the people of Israel that by the name of Jesus Christ of Nazareth, whom ye crucified, whom God raised from the dead, even by him doth this man stand here before you whole. This is the stone which was set at nought of you builders, which is become the head of the corner. Neither is there salvation in any other: for there is none other name under heaven given among men, whereby we must be saved" (Acts

4:10-12). Now we see Peter, acting according to his true capacities, no longer hobbled by fear. He refuses to be intimidated by anyone. Powerful as his captors are, they cannot extort actions from him through fear which he regards as execrable, which heretofore a child could wring from him. He is his own man now, never again to be ruled by fear.

Jesus, as we have seen, came in order to show us how we could achieve our God-given destiny. He gave us a teaching which, if followed, will engender in us certain fundamental moral attitudes toward life which will allow us to respond to the various challenges of life in a way which will lead to the development of our capacities along the lines of their authentic possibilities. Now since fear is one of the most powerful of the ways in which we respond to certain of life's situations, and since in a condition of morbidity it can become one of the most destructive forces in man's life, it was necessary that Jesus should also show us how we might deal with this problem. When we "let that mind be in us which was also in Christ Jesus," we see the world, ourselves, and others as Jesus saw them. Fear cannot so dominate us that our perception is distorted to the extent that we see the obstacles and difficulties which form a necessary part of our daily lives as "giants," and we ourselves as helpless "grasshoppers" before them. No, when we see things as Jesus did, when we have the Christ-mind in us, we may see difficulties on this side and that; enemies who would work our woe may surround us, but we remain unafraid since we have God's assurance that even though "a thousand shall fall at thy side, and ten thousand at the right hand . . . it shall not come nigh unto thee" (Psalm 91:7).

10 | And Smoking Flax Shall He Not Quench...

Matthew 12:20

All of us I suppost at some point in our passage on life's journey probably feel more or less that nothing describes our condition quite so accurately as the words of Francis Thompson in his well known poem *The Hound of Heaven* when he writes:

"I shook the pillaring hours
And pulled my life upon me; grimed with smears
I stand amid the dust O' the mounted years—
My mangled youth lies dead beneath the heap."

We feel bruised by the "slings and arrows of outrageous fortune," as Shakespeare calls them, wearied on life's way. We become keenly aware of our own shortcomings, the ways in which we have fallen so far short of the ideals which we had seen so clearly in our youth, At such moments the impulse to discouragement seems irresistible. It is at just such times as these that the words of the twelfth Chapter of St. Matthew's Gospel "A bruised reed shall he not break, and smoking flax shall he not quench," come as a healing balm to our troubled souls. At times such as these when we feel dejected and disheartened these words come to us as a great source of consolation. During such moments when we are so very painfully aware of our failures there is also a strong tendency to lose patience with ourselves.

We are all, I suppose, more or less aware of our faults of impatience with others. We fly off the handle, let fly a stream of biting words, and after we cool off are sorry for our lack of patience with our husband or wife, or child or friend. But how often do we ever stop to think about the unkindness which we do to ourselves? We are aware enough of the ways in which we hurt other people through the unkind hurting words which escape from us in a fit of impatience, and which we afterwards regret. How often are we aware of how shamefully we treat ourselves, and of the mean and hurting words which we use against oursleves in that interior dialogue of self-flagellation which takes place whenever we do something which doesn't exactly live up to our expectations of ourselves? It is a strange irony that all of us, I guess, feel a bit guilty that we're not really as unselfish toward our neighbor as we could be, and we're really a little bit too much concerned with "number one." The ironical part of it is, however, that we will feel great remorse over bitter, cutting words which we say to someone else, but over the mean, nasty things which we say to ourselves, we never have a second thought. In this case we are indeed failing to live up to the command of Jesus, but our failure is not at all the one which we usually think it is. Our failure is not keeping the command which Jesus gave us when he said, "Thou shalt love thy neighbor *as thyself*" (Matthew 19:19) . The problem for most people is this. Once in a great while, maybe, we treat others "like dirt." With ourselves, we do it all the time. If your wife or husband or friend makes a small mistake, "goofs" as we say, we overlook it, or perhaps it is even an occasion for a few laughs. If *we* make a mistake, regardless of how trifling, ah what an interior tirade ensues, what endless self-recrimination! "How could I have been so stupid!" "You idiot haven't you learned *anything* in 41 years!" And so on, and so on, and so on. We just can't forgive ourselves. If we ever said the things to our friends, or even to our enemies, that we say to ourselves we would be so ashamed that we wouldn't want to show our face in public again. Yet, it is not an exaggeration to say that these are the kinds of things that we say to ourselves every day of the week, and never even give it a second thought. Perhaps we would do well to reflect upon a poster which is enjoying some popular currency at the moment. It reads, "Be patient with me. God isn't finished with me yet." No doubt if we were to take this to heart we would be more forgiving of ourselves, more patient with ourselves, more tolerant of our failings and shortcomings. In a word, more loving.

We would realize that all of us are to a greater or lesser extent "bruised reeds." We are not yet perfect, but in need of the loving care of Jesus to regain our spiritual health. And this is exactly why Jesus came into the world. Jesus tells us in Luke's Gospel quoting the prophet Isaiah's description of the Savior who was to come, that his purpose in coming is to "bind up the broken heart" (Luke 4:18, Isaiah 61:1). If, as followers of Jesus, we wish to become more like him, then we must make our attitude more like his, not only our attitude towards others, but also our attitude towards *ourselves*. One thing is certain—Jesus would never say the mean, cruel things to you that you say to yourself. We have no difficulty in being convinced that if we wish to be more Christ-like, we should try to be more kind, more thoughtful, more loving toward our neighbor. It is, however, very difficult to convince people that they should not be so harsh to themselves; that they should not speak mean, nasty words to themselves when they make mistakes; and that just as they would feel that it was wrong if they failed in kindness and generosity and love toward their neighbor, that it is every bit as wrong to treat themselves this way.

When we are feeling dejected and disspirited because of our failings and imperfections then those words of the Gospel "the bruised reed he shall not break and the smoking flax shall he not quench," serve as a great source of consolation to us. This is why Jesus says, "the son of man is come to save that which was lost" (Matthew 18:11). Jesus illustrates this purpose of his in one of the most beautiful of his parables, that of the Good Shepherd. In Luke 15:4-7 Jesus likens his dealings with mankind to that of a shepherd who is truly solicitous for the welfare of his sheep. Such a shepherd is concerned not just for sheep in general. He is concerned for the welfare of each individual sheep. Indeed John tells us that he knows each sheep by name (John 10:3). So solicitous is he for the care of each sheep, that should one of them wander off on his own from the flock, the shepherd leaves everything to go and search for his straying sheep, and he does not rest until he finds him. Further, this Good Shepherd loves the sheep so much that if some danger threatens them, perhaps a pack of wolves, he will defend and protect them, even to the point of laying down his own life (John 10:11-15).

Jesus is teaching us in this parable of the Good Shepherd how God regards us and how he deals with us. The parable shows us not only God's love for us but also his patience with us. When the wayward sheep has wandered off on his own, far from the care of the shepherd, and becomes lost, the Good Shepherd does not react with anger. And when he, after having expended great energy and effort in trying to track down the vagrant sheep, finally finds it, far from being angry with it and excoriating it with opprobrious language, he offers it not a word of reproach. He doesn't say, "Now you're going to be sorry you went off on your wanderings"; or, "After I get done switching you within an inch of your life, I'll guarantee you that you won't go meandering off by yourself again," or anything of the sort. He doesn't utter a word of reproof. He understands how silly sheep are. After all, that's why they need a shepherd. If they had enough sense, they could fend for themselves. So the Good Shepherd doesn't scold the poor strayed sheep—he is too happy to have it back to spoil the reunion with pettifogging over trivial details.

Jesus declares he is the Good Shepherd. This means that all of those qualities which we have so much admired in the Good Shepherd in the parable characterizes Jesus in his dealings with his people. Just as the Good Shepherd is patient with the straying sheep, so also is Jesus with us. This means also that just as Jesus is patient with us and doesn't expect instant perfection in us, so also should we be patient with ourselves. But we must be constantly reminded of these qualities which God possesses and his attitude of love and patience toward us, because we tend very quickly to forget them. Or, having heard that God is thus, we file it away in some dusty corner of our minds, and then continue steadfastly in our conception of God as some kind of a Chairman of the Cosmic Watchdog Committee on Vice whose Argus-eyed vigilance no wrong escapes.

If one wanted to get some kind of an inkling about the way the average person thinks about God, it would be revealing to perform the following experiment. First, the experimenter would take a random grouping of "good Christians," and without in any way intimating what the purpose of the experiment was, he would ask the subjects of the experiment to write out a description of what the would consider to be a really ideal personality, one that they would most desire for themselves if they could change themselves in whatever way they most desired. No doubt there would be some variety in the personality characteristics that would be enumerated. It is very doubtful indeed, however, that *anyone* would put down that they thought an ideal person was one who is sneaky; who operates by stealth; who does his best to entrap people; who exacts the last drop of blood from all of his agreements with his friends; who is hard and unrelenting in all of his dealings with others; who is merciles and unforgiving. No one, but no one, would consider such a personality desirable.

The second part of our experiment would consist in this. Several months later, after our group had completely forgotten about the first phase of our experiment we would ask them to take a piece of paper and write out to the best of their ability what they thought God was like. The strange part of this experiment is that the features of the picture of God which emerged from these descriptions would consist of those qualities which they would find totally obnoxious in their own personalities. In other words, God's personality is made up, in the mind of the average person, of qualities such as sneakiness, unfriendliness, a desire to entrap and catch the unwary, a relentless pursuit of revenge on someone who has offended, cold and unsympathetic intolerance of weakness, etc., which he would not even tolerate in himself! If someone were asked to write a description of our own personality and it turned out to be like God's, we would be so crushed that we'd probably sit down and cry to think that people thought so badly of us!

One of God's major purposes in becoming man in Jesus was exactly this—to try to live down the bad reputation that He seemed to have acquired over the years. Or, expressed more seriously, the life of Jesus would reveal what God really is like, and that the God which is revealed in Jesus is love. Further, that God who is love, and out of love created us, since he made us, knows what we are like. He understands our weaknesses and our frailties; he understands the heights of devotion and self-sacrifice to which we can ascend; he knows the sublime generosity of which we are capable. And he also knows that we can be petty, childish, weak and all the rest. It was because of our weakness, because we were bruising our knees and elbows on the rocky path of life's way, because we had wandered astray into thorns that were tearing our flesh that he came, "to bind up the broken heart." The humanity which Jesus found was, and is, all bruised reeds, all smoking flax. Christ in his infinite widsom knows that if he forces the reed too much it will break. He realizes that to load too much fuel on the little spark which is smoldering in the flax will smother it. The reed must be treated gently, brought along slowly. The flax must be fanned little by little before it will burst into flames, a task which requires infinite pains, and unlimited patience.

Now since it is true that we do not come all perfect and ready-made, like some Athena sprung from Zeus' brow, growth to our full potential requires much patience, patience first of all on God's part who must lead us like headstrong sheep; patience on our own part as we realize that we are not perfect, but with God's care we will arrive at our appointed destination; and the patience which we must have with one another, since we are all in the same human condition. As we have seen, God surely has patience with us and not only is completely aware of our human frailty, but has a loving concern for it. We have also seen that just as God loves us, we are also to love ourselves, "Love your neighbor *as yourself,*" and if we have a proper, well ordered, God-like love of ourselves, we must also, just as God does, have patience with our infirmities and imperfections. But what we should also be very well aware of is that God requires not only that we be patient with Him as He works in us day by day, and not only that we be patient with ourselves in our slowness to respond to God's care for us, but that we also must be patient with one another. Jesus demonstrated the necessity of this patience with our neighbor in a very striking way with a parable. Peter asks Jesus how many times he should forgive his brother, if he offends against him, and with one of his typical bursts of enthusiasm, suggests a figure which seems more than generous, seven. To which Jesus replies, "I say not unto thee, Until seven times: but, Until seventy times seven" (Matthew 18:22). Well, this surely must have seemed a rather crushing blow to poor Peter who had probably thought that he was outdoing himself in generosity when he had suggested the figure of seven, which it must be admitted, was a dramatic improvement over what they had been taught in the Old Law, namely, "Eye for eye, tooth for tooth, hand for hand, foot for foot, burning for burning, wound for wound, stripe for stripe" (Exodus 21:24-25). Certainly, when Peter had suggested that he take *seven* stripes without retaliation he must have anticipated a response of hearty approbation for his generosity from Jesus. Instead, Jesus tells him to forgive not up till seven times, but up till seventy times seven, or that his forgiveness of his neighbor should be unlimited.

He then goes on to illustrate his teaching concerning the way we ought to forgive one another with a parable. He says that there once was a king who had a servant who owed him a tremendous sum, and was unable to settle his debt. The King therefore called the servant, and when he confessed that he had not the wherewithal to pay what he owed, the king commanded that he, his wife, and his children be sold into slavery and all his property confiscated. We are told that, "The servant therefore fell down and worshipped him, saying, "Lord, have patience with me, and I will pay thee all" (Matthew 18:26). The king, moved with compassion, forgave him his enormous debt and let him go. The servant, after he had departed from the king, encountered one of his fellow servants who owed him a trifling sum. He laid hold of the fellow and demanded immediate payment at which, "His fellow servant fell down at his feet and besought him, saying, Have patience with me and I will pay thee all" (18: 29). But he would not and cast him into prison until the last farthing of the debt be paid. His fellow servants, being outraged at his conduct, went back and reported it to his master. Angered by this flinty-hearted obdurateness in one who had himself asked for and received mercy, the King cast him into prison until the last penny was paid which he owed. The lesson which Jesus wishes us to learn from this parable is clear—"So likewise shall my heavenly Father do also unto you, if ye from your hearts forgive not everyone his brother their trespasses" (Matthew 18:35).

Here we encounter one of the most fundamental of all of Jesus' teachings, namely, the necessity of forgiving our enemies from our heart. Jesus, as we have seen, came that we might have a rich, full life. In order to have such a life, Jesus taught us certain basic attitudes which we ought to have toward life, such as a giving, generous spirit, a faith that sees all things as possible with God's help, a trust in God which makes anxiety for the future unnecessary, and so on. Of these fundamental attitudes toward life, clearly forgiveness of our enemies is one of the most important in the mind of Jesus. Jesus realized that so long as we hate our enemies and occupy our minds with thoughts of revenge, and strategies for getting even, our creative energies, which should be put to a much more constructive use, are being dissipated. Further, when I decide that I am going to seek any and every opportunity to avenge myself on my enemy, to that extent, I forfeit my freedom. I allow my enemy to control my behavior, so that he is able to do me a double hurt. First, he hurts me by the injustice which he inflicts on me, and second, by controlling my behavior, he forces me to put my freedom in his hands. When I decide to try to get back at him, I allow him to lead me around by the nose. My behavior is controlled by him.

Whereas when I forgive the injury which has been done to me I am free. Certainly someone might do me a wrong. But after he has done his best to hurt me, and indeed succeeded, if I refuse to occupy my time in scheming and laying plots for revenge, there is nothing more that he can do. I am free of him. If, however, I can't do that, if I can't let go until I get my pound of flesh, I am like a prisoner who has escaped from jail but is still handcuffed to the guard— I may have gotten out of jail but I am still not free, until I can get free from the guard to whom I am handcuffed. In a similar way I chain myself to my enemy, and make it possible for him to do me not just one wrong, but a second one as well. I make myself his slave, and he makes me serve him when I try to revenge myself upon him.

Jesus, of course, realized when one of our basic attitudes towards life is to be ever vigilant so that we repay every wrong that is done to us that we're going to be very busy indeed, and busy in a very unrewarding and unproductive way. Jesus, on the other hand, wanted us to be free, "Ye shall know the truth and the truth shall make you free" (John 8:32) . So by his teaching that we are to forgive our enemies from our heart Jesus shows us an attitude toward life that is crucially important to us in our quest for happiness. It was not one that the Apostles learned very easily though. Thus we read in St. Luke that as Jesus was on his way to Jerusalem he desired to stay in a Samaritan town but they would not receive him. James and John were outraged at this insult and said, "Lord, wilt thou that we command fire to come down from heaven, and consume them . . . ?" (Luke 9:54). They still had not learned the way of life that Jesus was trying to teach them, one of the most necessary parts of which was the forgiveness of our enemies. Jesus is therefore compelled to recall to their minds, "Ye know not what manner of spirit ye are of. For the Son of Man is not come to destroy men's lives but to save them." In order to make absolutely certain that the Apostles, and all of us who would follow him grasp just how essential this attitude of forgiveness is to the way of life which he was teaching, Jesus drove this point home to us as dramatically as he could, when in his dying moments, with his last gasp of breath, he forgave those who had wronged him so horribly.

Jesus came to teach us a way to approach life which will lead us to a rich and abundant life. He taught that in order to achieve this rich, abundant life certain fundamental attitudes are necessary, as we have seen. One of these attitudes is patience. We must be patient with ourselves, even when it seems we are making no progress at all and the sails of our spiritual bark droop listlessly and we seem to be becalmed on the sea of life. We must be patient with ourselves when in such moments we become painfully aware of our frailties and weaknesses, of how imperfectly we have thus far realized the ideals which Jesus proposes to us. We must be patient with our brothers and sisters who in their journey also experience the same weaknesses and imperfections that we do, and we must be patient when such weakness and infirmities cause us pain in our human interactions. And finally we must be patient with God, knowing that He also must proceed in us with infinite care and patience, lest by an overzealous haste, *He Quench The Smoking Flax.*